ADOPTION

A Legal Guide for Birth and Adoptive Parents

Kelly Allen Sifferman

Chelsea House Publishers

Philadelphia

1-99

First published in hardback edition in 1997 by Chelsea House Publishers.

1 3 5 7 9 8 6 4 2

Library of Congress Cataloging-in-Publication Data

Sifferman, Kelly Allen, 1956-
   Layman's law guides. Adoption / by Kelly Allen Sifferman.
     p. cm.
Rev. ed. of: Adoption. 2nd ed. c1994
Includes index.
   ISBN 0-7910-4438-6 (hc)
   1. Adoption—Law and legislation—United States—Popular works.
I. Sifferman, Kelly Allen, 1956- Adoption. II. Title.
   KF545.Z9s55 1997
346.7301'78—dc21   96-48967
                       CIP

ACKNOWLEGEMENTS

This book is dedicated to four special adoptive children: Alex, Jaime, Quinn, Gus, and all the other adoptive children, special in their own ways, who have crossed my path. Their happiness and the happiness of their birth and adoptive parents make practicing law more than a job. My thanks to Beverly Quidort, MSW, and Mary L. Verdier, former Juvenile Court Commissioner, for their constructive criticism of drafts of this book. Special thanks to Susan Sendrow who gently encouraged me to write this book. And most of all, thanks to my husband, and best friend, Mark, for always believing in me.

Kelly Allen Sifferman

TABLE OF CONTENTS

· ·

CHAPTER ONE
AN OVERVIEW OF ADOPTION . . . .

What is Adoption?

Every parent possesses certain rights and responsibilities to his or her child. The law grants these rights and imposes these responsibilities from the moment the child is born. These rights include the right of custody, the right to control, raise and educate the child, and the right to have the child inherit from the parent. The responsibilities include the duty to provide care and support to the child.

Adoption is the **legal** process by which these rights and responsibilities are given to a person to whom that child was not born. At the end of the adoption, the child's "biological parents" or "birth parents" no longer have any rights or responsibilities to the child. The "adoptive parents" now possess all the legal rights and responsibilities to the child, just as if that child had been born to them. After the adoption is finalized, the adoptive parents legally are the child's **"real parents."**

After the adoption is finalized, the adoptive parents legally are the child's "real parents."

If the legal process of adoption does not occur (or does not occur correctly), the legal rights and responsibilities of the birth parents are not ended. At the same time, the people with physical custody may not possess any legal rights to the child. All too often, great anxiety and sorrow results when people, although well intentioned, do not go through the formal adoption process and informally attempt to transfer the rights and responsibilities to a child.

There are many reasons why someone adopts a child. Perhaps a couple cannot conceive and bear a child themselves. In some cases, the child's mother has remarried and the stepfather wishes the child to "have his name." In other cases, a family wishes to share their life with a child with "special needs." Each situation is unique. Whatever the reason for the adoption, however, the legal procedure for the adoption is basically the same.

This book is written to explain the process to all those persons with an interest in adoptions, particularly parents who are contemplating placing or who have placed their child for adoption, persons who have adopted or are thinking about adopting, and those children who have been adopted and are inquisitive about their rights. Since some words have a technical meaning in the world of adoptions, there is a glossary at the end of this book to assist the reader.

The History of Adoption

Children have been adopted since ancient times. Probably the most famous adoption story in the western world comes from the Old Testament of the Bible. It is the story of Moses, an Israelite child who was adopted by an Egyptian princess who found the child in a basket in a river.

Although adoption has existed since ancient times, it is only in recent time that the law has formally recognized adoption. This fact distinguishes adoption from other areas of the law. Unlike contract law or personal injury law which have a long history of judge-decided law upon which they are based, adoption law is based almost entirely on statutes passed by legislatures.

In the United States, the first modern law recognizing adoption was passed in Massachusetts in 1851. Prior to that time, people changed custody of children informally without using the courts or transferred the rights and responsibilities to a child by a deed as if the child were a piece of property. Other states followed Massachusetts' lead and passed adoption laws which involved court proceedings and which are the close ancestors of today's laws.

Early adoption laws usually did not require any investigation or evaluation of the fitness of the potential adoptive parents. It was not until the end of the Nineteenth Century that states began to show concern for the welfare or "best interests" of the children who were being adopted. Michigan in 1891 was one of the first states to enact a law requiring that a judge make an investigation of the adoptive parents and child before finalizing an adoption. Later, states created agencies or required state officers to make the investigation for the judge.

Not until the end of the Nineteenth Century did states begin to show concern for the welfare of the children being adopted.

As a result of its historical roots, the adoption process is almost totally governed by laws passed by the fifty state legislatures. The exceptions include the adoption of Native American children or foreign children, where laws passed by the United States Congress apply.

Because the adoption process is governed by fifty state laws, the rules and procedures in one state may be different than the rules and procedures in another state. This book describes the rules and regulations **generally** applicable across the United States. Any person actually involved in an adoption, however, should consult a lawyer familiar with the laws of the state or states involved.

Who Can Adopt?

Most states allow any adult determined to be a "fit parent" to adopt.

Most states allow any adult determined to be a "fit parent" to adopt. Typically, the adoptive parents are a married couple. There is, however, no general rule against an **unmarried** person adopting.

Likewise, there is no **age** limit for adoptive parents. Nor is there any requirement that the parents have the same **race** or **religion** as the adoptive child.

These factors, such as marital status, age, race and religion, may affect whether a court finds the potential adoptive person a fit parent or determines the adoption to be in the "best interests" of the child (a topic discussed later). This should not discourage anyone from attempting to adopt, as courts today do not exhibit any general prejudice to those adoptive parents who are not young, married couples.

In practice, it is more difficult for single or older parents to be placed with a child. This occurs because most birth parents prefer to place their child with a two parent family or with people of the same ethnic or religious background. Also, many adoption agencies impose their own rules on adoptions they assist. Adoption agencies sometimes work primarily with a certain race or faith, or do not place children with people who are older, such as over forty-five years of age.

With this said, **it is not impossible** for single, older, or racially and religiously different persons to adopt. It just means that the wait for a child may be longer or the potential adoptive person may need to be flexible about the child he or she hopes to adopt. The more open a potential adoptive person is about the type of adoptive child he will adopt, the sooner it is that this parent will be placed with a child.

It is not impossible for single, older, or racially and religiously different persons to adopt.

Who Can be Adopted?

All states allow minors to be adopted. Some states, however, require that the child be at least a certain number of years younger than the adoptive parents.

Whether an adult may be adopted depends on the wording of the particular state's adoption statute. Even where a state allows an adult adoption, a court may deny the adoption if the relationship to be created is something other than a parent-child relationship.

CHAPTER TWO
TYPES OF ADOPTIONS

Agency Adoptions

Agency adoptions are adoptions which some type of agency handles. It is thought that adoption agencies evolved from orphanages. Traditionally the birth parents would give the child to the adoption agency. The agency then had the responsibility to place the child with the adoptive parents or keep custody of the child indefinitely. Adoption agencies in the United States today do not resemble orphanages. While the agency still will take the responsibility of finding adoptive parents for the child, usually either the birth parents or foster parents retain custody of the child until placement with the adoptive parents.

Most states have created and funded a department which handles adoptions. These agencies are called **public agencies**. Typically, these public agencies help in the adoption of children who, for one reason or another, have become wards of the state.

Public agencies help in the adoption of children who, for one reason or another, have become wards of the state.

In addition to public agencies, all states license **private agencies** to place children for adoption. Such private agencies often are identified with a religion or race. Christian Family Care, Jewish Family Services, Catholic Social Services, and Black Family Services are some examples. Sometimes, but not always, private agencies focus on the adoption of children with certain social or racial backgrounds.

All states allow **non-profit private agencies** to operate. In addition, some states permit **for profit adoption agencies**. Whether a for profit agency may operate in a state depends on the **licensing** statutes of that particular state. These licensing statutes allow state government to monitor and audit both non profit and for profit private adoption agencies to make certain that the agency complies with all the adoption laws. Generally, as a citizen, you are entitled to learn from the government department involved whether any adoption agency operating in your state is in compliance with the licensing laws.

Adoption agencies are aware of the many common pitfalls of adoptions and how to avoid them.

A major advantage of adoption agencies is that they usually have a great deal of experience in the adoption area and are aware of the many common pitfalls of adoptions and how to avoid them. Additionally, an agency will take much of the burden off the adoptive parents by being the "go between" for the adoptive and birth parents. For example, an agency will most likely have the means to handle a call from a birth mother in the middle of the night who is in labor and has no transportation to the hospital.

The agencies also have the means to provide needed services to both the birth parents and adoptive parents. These services may include adoption education and counseling for the adoptive parents and birth parents, the performing of a home study on the adoptive parents, making medical arrangements for the birth mother, matching the birth parents' child with the adoptive parents, obtaining the birth parents' consents to adoption or aiding with the termination of a birth parent's parental rights, placing the adoptive child in the adoptive home, performing the post placement investigation and helping with the legal finalization of the adoption.

Some public agencies do not provide these services themselves. Rather, they direct the birth parents and adoptive parents to other governmental programs which provide these services.

One substantial advantage of private agencies is that they perform many of these services under one roof, which is convenient and expedient for the adoptive parents as well as the birth parents. The disadvantage of some private agencies is that they have so many adoptive parents apply for their adoption programs that they must limit the number of adoptive parents they can select. They do this by setting certain criteria such as age of the adoptive parents or whether the adoptive mother will be working outside the home. Or perhaps an agency is set up to only work with adoptive parents of a certain religion. Adoptive parents who do not fit private agency criteria may have better luck working with a private attorney if they reside in a state where private agencies are permitted by law.

Adoptive parents who do not fit private agency criteria may have better luck working with a private attorney.

The adoption agency may use an attorney to obtain the written consent for adoption from the birth parents or to petition for a termination of the birth parents' parental rights to the child. Sometimes, the agency's lawyer works or talks with the birth parents or adoptive parents during the adoption process. The attorney even may explain the legal process and the parties' rights. But the agency and its attorney usually consider the attorney to be the agency's attorney, and not the attorney for either the birth parents or the adoptive parents.

It should be made clear and preferably put in writing who the attorney does and does not represent. If the agency attorney is not the lawyer for the birth parents or the adoptive parents, information given to the attorney by the birth parents or adoptive parents may not be protected by the attorney-client privilege.

Even when an agency is involved and the agency has its own lawyer, the adoptive parents usually need to hire their own lawyer for the actual adoption petition and hearing. In some areas of the country, this work is performed for free or at a reduced cost by the county attorney.

Attorney Adoptions

Agencies have become more sensitive to the needs of their clients. They strive to provide their clients as much input and involvement as possible into the adoption process; nevertheless, some adoptive and birth parents want to have direct control over their adoption without the agency structure. For these people, an attorney facilitated adoption (otherwise called a "private placement") may be the answer.

The attorney's role is to be a facilitator between the birth parents and the adoptive parents.

The role of an attorney in an attorney facilitated adoption is quite different than in an agency adoption. In these cases, the attorney not only has the responsibility for the legal aspects of the case, but is also responsible for its social aspects. The attorney's role is to be a facilitator between the birth parents and the adoptive parents. The attorney also will need to handle the financial aspects of the case, such as the payment of the birth mother's medical expenses. The attorney may have the task of locating the birth father to try to obtain his consent or to terminate his parental rights through the court.

Because of lawyers' ethical rules on conflicts of interests, generally there are two lawyers involved in an attorney facilitated adoption. One attorney represents the birth parents with the other lawyer representing the adoptive parents. As long as full disclosure is given and the birth parent's interests are truly served, the adoptive parents may (and usually do) pay the legal fees of the lawyer for the birth parents.

The adoptive parents may (and usually do) pay the legal fees of the lawyer for the birth parents.

The advantages of an attorney facilitated adoption include greater flexibility in meeting the requests of the birth and adoptive parents. If the birth parent wants to meet the adoptive parents numerous times before choosing them to adopt her child, then the attorney will try to accommodate her. If the adoptive parents want to videotape the birth of the child, this request can be made directly to the attorney or to the birth mother. An agency may not be able to provide this flexibility, but an attorney (assuming a competent one) always can.

A disadvantage of an attorney adoption is that it may be harder to arrange for the birth parents to get adoption counseling. All adoption attorneys should be aware of the importance of adoption education and counseling for their clients and be able to make referrals to counseling centers and agencies where this counseling may be obtained. But this referral system certainly is not as convenient for the client as in the agency setting.

Another disadvantage is that while all lawyers must be licensed, some may not be competent to work in the adoption area. Although the laws and procedures on adoptions are not extremely complex, some lawyers unfortunately attempt to work in the area without experience or without learning the laws and procedures. When an inexperienced lawyer is used, not only is there a chance the cost will increase, but the danger exists that some procedure is performed incorrectly or some law is violated, potentially invalidating the adoption.

Persons working with an attorney ought to learn the background and experience of the lawyer.

Just as persons working with adoption agencies ought to check the background of the agencies, persons working with an attorney ought to learn the background and experience of the lawyer. References can be sought from people who have adopted or placed a child for adoption previously. Sometimes the local court handling adoptions (either the juvenile or probate court) will know the names of the attorneys who handle most of the adoptions. Names of experienced adoption attorneys also can be obtained from the American Academy of Adoption Attorneys.

WARNING: Private attorney adoptions are not allowed in some states. A few states require that all adoptions not involving a relative be handled by an agency. Be sure to check with your Attorney General, juvenile court, or a licensed attorney in your state.

Relative Adoptions

Relative adoptions are adoptions where the child is related to the adoptive parent by blood or marriage. Step-parent adoptions are perhaps the most common example of a relative adoptions.

Generally speaking, a relative adoption is simpler than an agency or attorney adoption. Virtually all states allow the birth parents to place a child for adoption with relatives without agency involvement. In many states, the stepparent, uncle, aunt, or grandparent does not need to be certified, or approved, to adopt. Also the usual waiting period for the child to be in the adoptive home before the entry of the final decree of adoption may be entered (usually six months) does not apply. We shall explore relative adoption in greater detail in Chapter 7, *Special Case Adoptions.*

All states allow the birth parents to place a child for adoption with relatives without agency involvement.

CHAPTER THREE
GETTING INTO THE ADOPTION SYSTEM
· ·

The Adoptive Parents' Perspective

Is it really that important to work with an agency or an attorney? Yes. Even if the potential adoptive parents have found a birth mother on their own, they still should work with an agency or attorney to make sure that everything is done properly. Whenever a person is dealing with issues as important as family and children, it is well worth the expense involved to insure that all is done correctly. And indeed the time and expense spent at the beginning will more than make up for the time, worry, and expense if things go wrong.

Before beginning the search for a child to adopt, potential adoptive parents should give great consideration to what kind of child they are prepared to care for and love. Can they accept a child with correctable medical problems? Can they deal with an older child placement? Do they only want a newborn? Would they adopt a one month old? A six month old? A twelve month old? Are they willing to accept a child of a different racial or ethnic background? Can they care for a baby born to a mother with a drug problem or a child who is the product of incest?

> *Potential adoptive parents should give great consideration to what kind of child they are prepared to care for and love.*

It is true that the more open they are about the kind of child they are willing to adopt, the sooner hopeful adoptive parents will locate a child to adopt. However, potential adoptive parents must be honest with themselves and be sure that they can be the best parent for this child—whatever the child's needs.

Finding a Child to Adopt

There is no question that there are fewer infants to adopt than in the past. This appears to have resulted from the legalization of abortion, the availability of contraception, the decrease in the social stigma of unmarried women raising a child, and the availability of welfare for mothers. At the same time, there are more couples discovering that they are infertile. The dilemma for adoptive parents then is how to find a child to adopt.

Many potential adoptive parents choose to work with an agency so that the agency will find a child for them. The agency may have been contacted by birth mothers who have found the agency through referrals from social agencies, a church, a doctor, or a friend or classmate. Adoption agencies are listed in the yellow pages of the telephone book, and some agencies advertise for birth mothers on television or in newspapers.

As the number of babies to adopt becomes scarcer, many agencies encourage adoptive parents to work independently.

As the number of babies to adopt becomes scarcer, many agencies encourage adoptive parents to work independently in finding their adoptive child. There are several approaches. Some adoptive parents place ads in local and college newspapers. However, it is important to check the laws in the states where the advertisement appears. Advertising for birth mothers is legal in some states and illegal in others.

Another effective way to find birth parents is through family, friends or church. It is these types of connections which often result in the placement of a child. It is helpful then for people interested in adopting to let as many people know as they are comfortable telling that they wish to adopt.

It also is a good idea to contact the adoption attorneys in the area to express an interest in adoption. Birth mothers often contact adoption attorneys about placement and the attorney may be able to make a connection. Potential adoptive parents usually follow up an initial contact with a resume or flier.

Potential adoptive parents usually follow up an initial contact with a resume or flier.

One adoptive parent named Jan Walton sent out 301 resumes across the state of Arizona in June of 1991. A few weeks later, Jan and her husband learned that a birth mother, who had just delivered, had read their resume and selected them to adopt her baby. Jan now has begun a networking service called Adoption Beginnings to help other prospective adoptive parents find birth parents.

The Birth Parents' Perspective

It sometimes seems that it is easier for birth mothers to obtain information on abortion or on keeping their child than to receive useful and practical information on adoptions. While some social agencies have begun to make more of an effort to explain the option of adoption, birth mothers who are interested in adoption need to be persistent in asking questions of workers at social agencies. The birth mother should keep asking questions until she thinks she has been given all the information about adoption she needs. Birth mothers should not be afraid of repeating questions or even of asking the questions of some other worker or supervisor when the first social worker's response is not satisfactory.

If a birth mother can not receive sufficient adoption information from the social agency, she ought to try another social agency. The birth mother also might consult directly with an adoption agency or adoption attorney. Most telephone directories have a separate listing for adoption in the yellow pages. Attorneys and adoption agencies place their names and telephone numbers in this section.

Besides referrals drawn from the yellow pages, the single most important referral source for birth mothers is word of mouth. Either the birth mother has a friend who placed a child for adoption with this agency or that attorney, or the referral comes from the obstetrician, a hospital nurse, or the hospital social worker. These are the people who come in contact with birth mothers and who also know the attorneys or agencies who work in the adoptions area.

A birth parent is free to interview agencies or attorneys and get information without committing to placing a child for adoption.

It is important for a birth parent to understand that by consulting with an adoption agency or attorney, the birth parent has not committed herself to placing her child for adoption with this agency or attorney, or even committed to placing the child for adoption at all. Not until the legal written consent paperwork is signed (usually after the child's birth) **and this consent becomes final** has the birth parent made a irrevocable legal commitment to place the child for adoption. Therefore a birth parent is free to interview agencies or attorneys and get as much information as needed about the adoption process without committing to placing a child for adoption.

Just as adoptive parents need to ask themselves what they desire in a child, a birth parent needs to (and has the ability to) ask herself what **she wants** in an adoptive family for her child. For instance, does she want her child to have siblings? Does she want a two parent family? Or is a single parent O.K.? Does she want the parents to live in her home state or out of state? Is it important that the family practice her religion? Does it matter that the mother works outside the home or does she want a stay-at-home-mom? Does she want to meet the adoptive family? Does she want to have periodic updates on the child in the future? Does she want to meet with the adoptive parents and child after the adoptive placement? Does she want to place no restrictions or qualifications on the placement of her child?

After the birth mother has thought about these things, she needs to convey her thoughts and desires to the adoption agency or attorney with whom she is working. This allows the agency or attorney to **match** the birth with adoptive parents.

The Match

Before the adoption process proceeds, the birth parents must agree to place their child with specific potential adoptive parents and those adoptive parents must agree to have the child placed with them. Once both sides agree, it is said that the birth parents and the adoptive parents are **matched**.

To accomplish a match, the adoption agency or attorney must possess enough information about the birth parents and the adoptive par-

Once both sides agree, it is said that the birth parents and the adoptive parents are matched.

19

ents to make an informed judgment about which birth parents and which adoptive parents are likely to agree to the placement of the child between them. Usually the adoption agency or attorney will present information to the birth parent about three or four adoptive parents who meet the birth parents' requests. These adoptive parents should have been told of the birth parents beforehand (including social and medical history) and asked whether they wish to be considered by the birth parents.

Most agencies and attorneys have "profiles" or "resumes" of adoptive families. These profiles can be anything from standardized questionnaire forms to elaborate photo albums. The purpose of these profiles is to give the birth parent enough information about the adoptive parents so that she feels comfortable with them adopting her child. Or the profile may make the birth parent interested enough to request more information about the adoptive parents.

Adoptive parents need to determine if the agency or attorney will allow a match with more than one birth parent at a time.

Adoptive parents need to determine if the agency or attorney with whom they are dealing will allow them to be matched with more than one birth parent at a time. Some agencies or attorneys match adoptive parents with only one birth parent at a time. Those adoptive parents with only one match may have missed a placement with another birth mother if the birth parent with whom they are matched changes her mind after the match.

Changing Minds after the Match

The birth parent **can legally change her mind** after the match. Until a consent to adopt is signed and becomes irrevocable under the law, the birth parent can decide to place the child with someone else or decide not to place the child for adoption at all. Potential adoptive parents who have been matched must prepare themselves for this possibility as it happens often.

Placing a child for adoption is one of the most difficult things a person can do. A birth mother may believe that placing her child for adoption is the best thing for the child and herself, yet when the time comes for the actual placement, she can not follow through. There is truly no way to absolutely predict that **this** particular birth mother, in fact, will place her child for adoption. Experienced adoption agencies and attorneys, however, sometimes can identify matches which probably will not be completed. Once advised, adoptive parents may decide to take the risk that the match will not result in placement in the hope that the birth mother places the child.

The possibility of a failed match is one of the realities of adoption. Some adoptive parents try to protect themselves from this possible disappointment by not telling their family and friends of the possible placement. Others need the support of their family and friends, and therefore tell them of the match. Each adoptive parent needs to decide what is best for him or her.

Besides the emotional risk of a failed match, adoptive parents also have a financial risk.

Besides the emotional risk of a failed match, adoptive parents also have a financial risk. Authorized living expenses, medical expenses, and counseling expenses are usually paid by the matched adoptive parents before the birth of the child. If the birth parent decides not to place the child , the adoptive parents may never be reimbursed those costs. Courts do not force birth parents to refund these expenses advanced by the adoptive parents.

The costs of these "failed matches" are a hidden cost of adoption. In budgeting (from both a financial and time standpoint) for an adoption, adoptive parent should consider that the first "match" with a birth mother may not result in an adoption. For this reason, some adoptive parents prefer to work with an agency where there is usually one fee paid regardless of how many "matches" it takes to result in an adoptive placement.

The adoptive parents also **legally may decide not to adopt the child** after the match. Of course, adoptive parents changing their minds happens much less often than a birth parent changing her mind.

Matched adoptive parents may change their minds after reviewing more detailed background information about the birth parents or after meeting with birth parents. Or the child may be born with some physical or mental condition.

Adoptive parents need to be comfortable with the match and need to be certain that they can be a good parent to the child.

Adoptive parents need to be comfortable with the match even after it is initially made and need to be certain that they can be a good parent to the child. The adoptive parents need to make these decisions for themselves.

The Certification Process

In order to adopt a child, adoptive parents must undergo some sort of scrutiny to determine whether they will be suitable parents. This scrutiny results in what is called the **"Home Study."**

In some states, a written home study is prepared and presented to the court. The court will review the home study and **certify** whether the adoptive parents are acceptable or non acceptable to adopt children.

In other states, such as New York, Massachusetts, and Washington, a licensed agency or social worker prepares the home study report and also determines whether the adoptive parents are suitable parents. In these states, the court does not review the home study.

Potential adoptive parents should start this certification process early, even before being matched with a birth parent. Being certified increases the chances of an early match and placement. Some states limit or prohibit even the temporary placement of children with people who are not certified or are not foster parents.

Some states limit or prohibit even the temporary placement of children with people who are not certified.

Even though the process by which adoptive parents are certified as suitable to adopt may differ from state to state, the content of the home study is generally the same throughout the country.

Most home studies deal with the following issues:

- Are the adoptive parents financially secure?

- Is the adoptive couples' marriage secure and stable?

- Do the adoptive parents have other children?

- Are the adoptive parents current in their support obligations to their other children?

- Do the adoptive parents have a stable job and life?

- Have the adoptive parents ever been arrested?

- Have the adoptive parents ever been reported for child abuse?

- Are the adoptive parents in good physical and mental health?

- What is the adoptive parents' home like?

- What kind of child are the adoptive parents hoping to adopt?

- Why do the adoptive parents wish to adopt?

- Do the adoptive parents' friends and family support the adoption?

If the investigation results in a **negative home study** and a recommendation that the potential adoptive parents not be allowed to adopt, the home study may be appealed. The appeal process will vary from state to state.

Once the certification to adopt has been granted, the approval usually remains in effect for one year.

Once the certification to adopt has been granted, the approval usually remains in effect for one year or until adoption, which ever occurs first. The certification approval usually can be extended for another year if the extension is requested before the approval expires.

Information Available to Birth Parents and Adoptive Parents

The birth parents and the adoptive parents may receive and are entitled to receive information about each other before the match and the placement. What information they are entitled to know about each other before match and placement depends on the laws and rules of the state involved.

Unless the parties have agreed to an **open adoption** (discussed in Chapter 11), the laws generally provide that **non-identifying information** about social and medical backgrounds are to be exchanged. Identifying information includes names, addresses and other information that specifically identifies the person.

Adoptive parents should receive, at a bare minimum, non-identifying information about the birth parents and the child. This information should include a social history as well as a medical history. Ideally the agency or attorney working with the adoptive parents should provide this information **before** the match or placement of the child.

Adoptive parents should receive non-identifying information about the birth parents and the child.

A sample questionnaire, set forth in Appendix A, illustrates what questions are typically asked of the birth parents. Agencies or attorneys may have their own form of background information, but most will ask similar types of questions of the birth parents.

CHAPTER FOUR
ALLOWABLE ADOPTION COSTS

Each state has laws covering the types of items for which the adoptive parents may pay. No state allows the birth parent to be paid for the child. Buying or selling a child is a serious criminal offense.

The adoptive parents, however, may provide certain financial assistance to the birth parents. Laws on financial assistance are enforced strictly to make sure that the claimed financial assistance is not really payment for the child in disguise.

> *Laws on financial assistance are enforced strictly to make sure that the financial assistance is not really payment for the child in disguise.*

As a general rule, most states allow adoptive parents to pay reasonable attorney fees for the adoptive parents and the birth parents, as well as any agency fees, and adoption counseling fees. Most states also allow the adoptive parents to pay the birth mother's medical expenses associated with the pregnancy and delivery of the child.

When dealing with the **medical expenses**, it is important that these expenses relate to the birth and delivery of the child. It may not be acceptable to pay for a birth mother's root canal unless a doctor were able to say that the root canal was necessary to her health and well being during her pregnancy. As another example, it may not be allowable for the adoptive parents to pay for the mother's tubal ligation as this expense is not related to her pregnancy or delivery.

Whether adoptive parents may pay **living expenses** of the birth parents depends on the law of the state involved. Living expenses may include :

- Food

- Maternity clothes

- Automobile gas

- Gas, electricity, water payments

- Telephone

- Housing

- Lost wages

The states differ wildly on their laws relating to birth mother's living expenses. Some states forbid payment of any living expenses. Some states allow the payment of reasonable and necessary living expenses during the pregnancy if these expenses have been pre-approved by the court. Other states are more lenient and even allow a payment to assist the birth mother after birth of the child.

Before adoptive parents pay a birth mother any living expenses, they should find out what expenses are allowable in the state involved. Waiting to find out before paying is not always easy to do. It is very difficult **not** to help a birth mother who may be facing eviction or having her heat turned off unless she gets money now. But it must found out what can be done under the law. It will not help the situation to go outside the law; it will only add more problems to an already difficult situation.

Accepting or providing financial help which is **not allowed** by applicable state law may subject the birth parent and the adoptive parents to criminal charges. And a court may not approve the adoption if there was an improper payment.

An itemized report or accounting (usually under oath) detailing the amounts paid by the adoptive parents may need to be filed with the court at or before the adoption hearing. Such reports may need to include not only amounts actually paid, but also amounts promised to be paid, and the disclosure of anything of value which is given, or promised to be given in an adoption. The court reviewing the report may or may not allow these expenses, may limit the amounts, or even disallow the adoption where the amounts are excessive.

An itemized report detailing the amounts paid by the adoptive parents may need to be filed with the court.

The bottom line is, check with an attorney or agency to find out exactly what adoption expenses are allowed.

Medical Insurance

Generally, the adoptive parents can pay for the medical expenses related to the pregnancy and birth of the child. In some instances, the birth mother has her own insurance or is covered by government programs. In that situation, the adoptive parents are not responsible for the medical expenses.

However, in many cases, the birth mother has no insurance and is not enrolled in any government programs. Here, the adoptive parents may guarantee payment to the mother's medical providers. This is a tricky area, because if the adoptive parents are guaranteeing payment of the medical expenses, they may be financially responsible **even if the mother decides not to place her child for adoption**. This may be an acceptable risk for the adoptive parents, but the adoptive parents must be made fully aware of the risk.

Some states have now enacted insurance legislation requiring that if an adoptive parent's insurance policy has maternity benefits, then this insurance must cover their birth mother's medical expenses just as if the child had been born to them. The insurance companies, however, have very strict notice requirements. These requirements must be followed exactly in order for the coverage to apply. Therefore, it is very important that the adoptive parents do the following:

Insurance companies' notice requirements must be followed exactly in order for coverage to apply.

1) Contact their insurance company to see if they cover birth mother's medical expenses and/or the child's medical expenses. If the company employee advises that coverage exists, determine the name of the individual providing the coverage information and confirm this coverage by writing a letter to the insurance company;

2) As soon as the adoptive parents have become certified or approved to adopt a child, they should notify their insurance company in writing about the certification;

3) Once a birth mother has been identified as planning on placing her child with them, the adoptive parents should notify their insurance company in writing of the birth mother's expected due date;

4) Notify the insurance company by phone, and in writing, once the child is born, and let the insurance company know if the child has any special needs;

5) Finally, notify the insurance company by phone and in writing once the child is in the adoptive parents' home.

Remember! The insurance company has no obligation to pay any medical expenses if the adoptive placement does not occur. Yet the adoptive parents may be liable to pay these expenses, if they have guaranteed these expenses, even if the adoption does not take place.

The insurance company has no obligation to pay medical expenses if the adoptive placement does not occur.

CHAPTER FIVE
WHAT HAPPENS AT THE BIRTH OF THE CHILD?

Before the birth mother goes to the hospital, she should call her attorney or adoption agency to let them know. They can do much to smooth the way for the birth mother with the hospital if any help is needed.

When the birth mother is admitted in the hospital, the hospital will want to know who will be responsible for the birth mother's medical bill. If the birth mother is covered under her own insurance or by government assistance, the birth mother will need to bring her insurance card with her. If the birth mother is a "private pay," then either the birth mother or another responsible party (usually the adoptive parents or adoption agency) will be financially responsible for the bill. It is important that the birth mother have this question resolved before she goes to the hospital.

The birth mother may have anyone she wants in the delivery room with her so long as the doctor and hospital approve. **The birth mother should talk with her doctor about this before the delivery**.

The birth mother may have anyone she wants in the delivery room with her so long as the doctor and hospital approve.

Some birth mothers want to have the adoptive mother with them during delivery. It has worked out well in some cases, but the birth mother must talk to the adoptive parents about this ahead of time to make sure this is something with which they are comfortable.

In many cases, having the adoptive parents present during the delivery makes it possible for them to bond with the baby right away. Having the adoptive parents there gives the birth mother the opportunity to share in their joy. Some adoptive parents feel it is too great a risk to allow themselves to bond with the baby before the consents have been signed. Other adoptive parents are uncomfortable with the intimacy of the setting. They need to do what feels comfortable to both them and the birth mother.

Some adoptive parents feel it is too great a risk to bond with the baby before the consents have been signed.

After delivery, the birth mother may see, hold, and feed the baby. This is the birth mother's baby and until the consent to adoption is signed, the birth mother has every right to that child. The birth mother does not **have** to see the baby if she does not want to. If it is uncomfortable for the birth mother to have a room on the maternity floor, she should talk with the her doctor ahead of time to see if she can get a room in another part of the hospital.

If the hospital has a social worker, this social worker will visit the birth mother to make sure the birth mother is doing well. Many times the hospital social worker will want to know whether the birth mother has had adoption counseling or at least had the opportunity to receive counseling. The social worker is only trying to help the birth mother through a possibly rough time in her life, but if the birth mother is not appreciative of these services, the birth mother has no obligation to talk with the social worker.

If the birth mother's adoption is confidential, she may not want anyone to know that she is in the hospital delivering. The hospital will respect the birth mother's privacy and not let anyone know that the birth mother is there. Understand however, the hospital will not let the birth mother's attorney or agency know where the birth mother is either, so if the birth mother wants them to know that she has delivered, she will need to contact them.

The birth mother is legally able to name the baby and receive a copy of the original birth certificate. **Once the adoption is finalized, the birth certificate will be changed to reflect the child's adopted name and the names of the adoptive parents as the parents.** The birth mother will not receive a copy of this amended birth certificate.

The birth mother can go home from the hospital as soon as she and her doctor feel she is ready. In many instances, the mother will be discharged before it is time to sign a consent to adoption. In this situation, the baby can go home with the birth mother, stay in the hospital, be placed in a temporary foster home (or receiving home) or go home with the adoptive parents.

If the birth mother does not agree to have the adoptive parents present at the birth of the child, the adoptive parents probably will not be contacted until after the baby is born. At that time they are typically told the sex of the child, the time and date of birth, the baby's weight and length, and how the baby and birth mother are doing.

Whether the adoptive parents can see the baby in the hospital depends on how open the adoption is.

Whether the adoptive parents can see the baby in the hospital depends on how open the adoption is. If it is a fairly open adoption, the birth parents will often want the adoptive parents at the hospital to feed the baby and to start bonding with the baby. Other birth mothers will want this time alone with the baby.

If the baby goes home with the adoptive parents before the consent to adoption is signed, the adoptive parents should check with their attorney or agency to determine whether the birth mother needs to sign a legal document giving them permission to take the baby home. An example of such a document appears on the following page.

MEDICAL AND SURGICAL AUTHORIZATION

Re: _____
(Name of Child)

(Expected) Date of Birth: _____

Adopting Parent(s): _____

The undersigned, being the birth parent of the above named child, authorize and empower the adopting parents shown above to make any provision for medical and surgical care for said child, including anesthesia, drug panel testing and/or autoimmune deficiency testing which may be deemed necessary or advisable by any licensed physician.

If this Authorization is signed before the birth of the child, it shall be valid as of the time that the adopting parents have actual custody of the child, or until this Authorization is superseded by adoption of the child.

A copy of this Authorization shall have the same effect as the original.

I hereby acknowledge receipt of a copy of this Medical and Surgical Authorization.

Dated : _____

Signed: _____
Birth Mother

SUBSCRIBED AND SWORN before me this___ day of_____ , 199__

by: _____
Notary Public

_____
Street Address

_____
City, State and Zip Code

My commission Expires:

_____

If the adoptive parents take the child home before the consent to adoption is final, they must understand that the birth parents may change their minds and ask that the child be returned to them. If the adoptive parents decide to take the baby home from the hospital before the consent is final, they must be prepared to take this risk.

At the time of the discharge of the child and placement of the child with the adoptive parents, they should receive newborn information. A sample form on the following page illustrates the type of information they typically should receive.

NEWBORN INFORMATION

Sex of child _____ Full term? _____

Date of birth _____ Premature (weeks) _____

Time of birth _____ Size of head _____

Weight at birth _____ Size of chest _____

Length at birth _____ Apgar score _____

Place of birth _____ Oxygen given?_____

Delivery:_____ Vaginal _____ Forceps _____ C-Section _____ Induced

Complications at birth, including any birth injury to child:

_____

_____

Medications given during hospital stay:

_____

_____

Physical defects noted (please specify):

_____

_____

Special notes:

_____

_____

How long in the hospital? _____

Breast fed? Yes _____ No _____ If yes, how long? _____

Formula type _____ Last feeding _____

Ounces consumed _____ Discharge weight _____

Recommended feeding schedule _____

39

CHAPTER SIX
THE LEGAL PROCEDURE FOR ADOPTION

• •

Consent

In many adoptions, one or both of the birth parents agrees to the adoption. In such cases, the birth parent or birth parents will sign a **consent** form. By this consent, the birth parent agrees to the termination of her parental rights to the child and agrees to the adoption.

Each state has its own form of consent to adoption and its own laws governing when a consent is signed. An example of a *Consent to Adoption* form used in Arizona can be found in Appendix B.

There are several characteristics which are common to all forms of consents. **The consent must be in writing**. An oral promise to place a child is not sufficient. (Florida is the only exception to this rule. It allows that a consent may be oral if made in court)

The consent must be signed voluntarily. The birth parent cannot be forced or tricked into signing the consent. The consent must be signed before witnesses, a notary public, or a judge.

When the consent involves a newborn, there usually is some time period which must pass before the consent may be signed.

When the consent involves a newborn baby, there usually is some time period after the birth of the child which must pass before the consent may be signed. In many states, to be valid, the consent can not be signed until 72 hours have passed from birth.

Washington is one state, however, that allows for a consent to be signed **before** the birth of the child. In the state of Washington, a birth parent may sign a consent anytime before the birth of the child, but the birth parent then has 48 hours following the birth to notify the attorney, adoption agency or court that she is not going to proceed with the adoption plan.

States differ on whether minors may consent to the adoption of a child without their parents' knowledge or approval. Some states require that the minor's parent consent to the adoption. For example, in Minnesota, the consent of an unmarried birth parent under age 18 also requires the consent of her parents or guardian. The New Hampshire Adoption Act states that the court may require the consent of a parent or legal guardian for an unwed mother who is under 18.

Other states simply require the minor's parent to be aware of the adoption plan. Still other states do not require any involvement by the minor's parents, but will require that a guardian be appointed to represent the minor birth parent. Finally there are states which allow a minor to give a consent to adoption without the knowledge or permission of her parents.

Whether a birth parent may change her mind after signing is probably the most misunderstood area of adoption law.

All the states require the consent of the child to be adopted if she is a over a certain age. The age varies from age 10 to 14 years.

Revoking a Consent to Adopt

Whether a birth parent may change her mind after signing a consent to adopt is probably the most misunderstood area of adoption law. This confusion exists because the rules on revoking a consent differ drastically among the states and much inaccurate information is communicated to birth parents and adoptive parents.

There is one basic universal rule. A birth parent may revoke a consent which was obtained by fraud or by the use of improper or illegal promises.

Outside of fraud and improper promises, the rules vary from state to state. In most states, such as Arizona and Massachusetts, once the consent is signed, it can not be taken back. Other states set a short period for revocation. Georgia, for example, allows a birth parent to change her mind within ten days of the consent signing.

A birth parent may revoke a consent which was obtained by fraud or improper promises.

Finally, there are other states where a birth parent may cancel the consent at any time before the adoption hearing. Since final adoption hearings sometimes do not occur until six months or more after the consent is signed, the adoptive parents may have custody for a substantial period of time with the risk that the birth parent may revoke the consent.

Placement

By signing the consent, the birth parent gives up custody of the child. The adoptive parents then take physical custody of the child. When this happens, a **placement** occurs. Adoptive placement of older children may occur at an adoption agency, a social agency, the adoptive parent's home, or any convenient place.

The placement of a baby being adopted may occur at the hospital. Many times, the birth mother may be present and actually place the baby in the arms of the adoptive parents. In other situations, the birth mother may have already checked out of the hospital.

Wherever the placement of a baby, the adoptive parents should be prepared. They should have clothes for the baby, a receiving blanket, and a car seat.

Temporary Custody Hearing

If an adoptive placement occurs before the adoptive parents are certified or approved to adopt, the court will require a hearing to ensure that the adoptive parents can provide proper care of the child pending the approval process. Usually this hearing is called a temporary custody hearing. The petition for temporary custody must be filed with the court soon after the placement and the hearing usually is set very quickly.

At the temporary custody hearing, the judge will inquire whether the home appears safe and suitable for the child.

At the temporary custody hearing, the judge will inquire whether a caseworker has visited the prospective adoptive home and whether the home appears safe and suitable for the child. Further, the judge will want to know if the caseworker anticipates certifying the petitioners as suitable adoptive parents. The judge is going to ask the petitioners whether they are in the process of becoming certified, whether they have ever been convicted of a misdemeanor or felony, or whether there has been any referral made against them to a child protective agency.

If, after hearing all the evidence, the judge feels the child will be safe in the petitioners' home, the judge will give the petitioners permission to have temporary custody of the child and authorize them to sign for any medical, dental, and surgical treatment by doctors, dentists and hospitals as well as sign for any educational, social and recreational services for the child. Once the petitioners become certified or approved to adopt, then the petitioners can file the petition to adopt.

If after hearing all the evidence the judge feels the child should **not** be in the petitioners' home, then the child will be removed immediately from the home. At this point the petitioners can appeal the decision, but the child will not be returned to them unless they win on the appeal.

Birth Father's Rights

Many birth mothers and adoptive parents make the mistake of ignoring a birth father's rights. Many people assume that the birth father has fewer rights than the birth mother. **This is not so!** The birth father has the same rights and responsibilities to the child as does the birth mother.

The birth father has the same rights and responsibilities to the child as does the birth mother.

The birth father has rights even if the birth parents are not married to each other, even if the birth father is in prison, and even if the birth father lives in another state or country. Also, the birth father has rights even if the birth mother is married to someone else. Whoever is the birth father, he must be given notice of and a voice in the adoption. There are very narrow exceptions to this rule; the first exception is in the case of the "unknown father."

Unknown Father

In this situation, the mother does not have enough information about the father to know who he is. Perhaps she met him one night while out partying. Or perhaps, in a tragic situation, she was raped by an unknown man.

Whatever the situation, the court will require sufficient details to make sure that the mother's story is credible and that she truly does not know the identity of the father before allowing the adoption to proceed. In fact, some judges require the mother to appear in court in an "Order to Show Cause" hearing and explain to the judge why the birth father's identity is unknown to her.

Sometimes a birth mother is uncertain who the father is because she had sexual relations with two or more men around the time it is thought the baby was conceived. This is another version of the unknown father situation. The courts usually handle this situation by letting all the possible fathers know of the adoption, so that each father will be given the chance to become involved in the child's life or adoption plan.

Very few courts allow a mother to refuse to identify a father.

Mother Refuses to Testify

The second exception to the rule is in the case where the birth mother refuses to identify the father. This is an extremely limited exception. Very few courts allow a mother to refuse to identify a father and those courts who do allow it will make sure that the mother has a very good reason for her refusal. Reasons such as the mother being "embarrassed" to reveal the father's name, or that he is a married man and the birth mother does not want his wife to find out are not sufficient reasons.

Indeed, the only time this exception can be used is when the mother is afraid of the birth father and he has told her that he would harm her if she involves him in the adoption. Even in this extreme situation, it is helpful if the birth mother has evidence to back up her story, such as medical records evidencing that she has been hurt by this man, or testimony of family or friends who can corroborate her claim.

Father's Whereabouts Unknown

In the third exception, the father's identity is known, but his whereabouts are unknown. In this situation, a diligent search must be made for the father. Some courts require that a contact be made with the father's friends and family. Records, such as voter's registration, driver's license, court files, directory assistance and utility records, may need to be searched.

In some instances the man the birth mother believes to be the father does not believe that he is the father. Instead of signing a consent, the **man then may sign a written denial of paternity**, and in doing so, agree that the adoption may proceed.

Under the law, the birth mother's husband is presumed to be the father of the child.

Finally there is the situation where the mother is married to one man, yet the birth father of the child is another man. Under the law, the birth mother's husband is presumed to be the father of the child **even if he is not the birth father.** In these situations, consents should be obtained from the actual birth father and the husband.

Because of the birth father's rights, the birth father must agree to place the child for adoption or he must be given the opportunity to parent his child. Without the consent of the birth father, an adoption can not proceed unless the birth father has his parental rights ended or terminated.

Termination of Parental Rights

When either one or both birth parents does not sign a consent, a procedure to terminate parental rights must be followed, and must be completed before an adoption is finalized. Refer to Appendix B for an example of a *Petition to Terminate Parental Rights* used in Arizona.

The specific, technical grounds for termination vary among the states. The usual grounds are unfitness, abuse or abandonment.

Judges are extremely reluctant to terminate a parent's rights. It is not enough to simply show that the child might be better off with someone else as a parent. Actual unfitness of or abandonment by the birth parent must be shown.

In every termination case, there must be a court hearing and the birth parent must be given notice of that hearing.

In every termination case, there must be a court hearing and the birth parent whose rights may be terminated must be given notice of that hearing. Courts generally will provide a lawyer to any birth parent who can not afford an attorney.

At the court hearing, the court must be convinced that the parent has abandoned the child or is unable to parent the child. Also, the court must be convinced that it is in the **child's best interests** that the parental rights be ended.

In the adoption context, it is usually the birth father whose rights are being terminated and the most commonly alleged ground for termination is abandonment. Even where the father's identity and whereabouts are unknown, the father must be provided with notice of the proceedings. Every effort must be made to locate the father so that he might be given personal notice of the termination hearing.

Every effort must be made to locate the father to give personal notice of the termination hearing.

If, after a thorough search, the father cannot be found, then the notice can be given to the father by publishing a notice of the termination hearing in a newspaper in the area where the father was last known to live. The notice is published also where the termination hearing is being held.

The Adoption Petition and Hearing

After the child has been placed with the adoptive parents, the parents may have been awarded temporary custody of the child or been declared guardians of the child. This means that the adoptive parents have the right to physical control of the child and have the right to consent to necessary medical procedures and social, athletic, and educational activities, as well as the responsibility to provide proper care and support for the child. But they are not the legal parents of the child.

To become legal parents of the child, an adoption hearing must be held. The adoption process is begun by the filing of an adoption petition. This petition is generally filed with the court along with either the consents of the birth parent or a court order terminating the birth parent's parental rights.

The adoption petition typically includes the names, ages and addresses of the adoptive parents and child; the relationship between the petitioners and child; the legal basis for termination of parental rights (that is, that the birth parents have consented to the adoption or that their rights have been terminated); that the adoptive parents are appropriate persons to adopt the child and that the adoption is in the child's best interests.

By way of example, we have included in Appendix B a sample *Petition to Adopt*, used in Arizona. This document will vary in form from state to state, but the contents of this document are fairly standard throughout the country.

The adoption hearing is generally held six months to a year following the placement of the child.

Once the petition to adopt is filed with the court, a date will be set for the adoption hearing. The adoption hearing is generally held six months to a year following the placement of the child with the adoptive parents.

There is a reason for the delay between the placement of the child with the adoptive parents and the final adoption hearing. This delay gives the adoptive parents and child the chance to bond and grow together as a family. Also, during this time period the family will be visited by a caseworker. The caseworker's job is to make sure the family is doing well and that the child is thriving in the adoptive home. If the adoptive parents have any questions or concerns, they should discuss them with the caseworker during this time.

The caseworker prepares a written report on the adoptive parents and the child's progress.

This report is usually reviewed by the court before or at the adoption hearing.

As a general rule, the adoption hearing is held in the state where the adoptive parents live. Some states like Washington allow the adoptive parents to finalize their adoption in the state where the child was born even if the adoptive parents live in another state or even another country.

The adoption hearing should result in a written order of the court. By this document, the child will become the legal child of the adoptive parents and the child's name legally will be changed to the name the adoptive parents have chosen. Once this order is signed by the judge, the adoption is **finalized**.

The Best Interests of the Child

In approving the adoption, the court must find that the adoption is in the child's best interests. Usually, there is no problem in proving this factor.

There are situations where the specific facts involved raise a question as to the child's "best interests." A court may determine that the characteristics or needs of the child are not compatible with the adoption by a single parent or by an older couple. Or the court may question whether these parents have the training, stamina or money to care for a child requiring special care.

If a child has been raised in one religion, placement with parents of another religion or no religion may be found to be too disruptive for the

In approving the adoption, the court must find the adoption to be in the child's best interests.

child. The best interest test also has been used to deny the adoption of a child by gay or lesbian couples.

Race sometimes is used as a "best interests" factor. Some states have a policy that children who are wards of the state preferably should be placed with parents of the same ethnic background. Constitutional challenges have been leveled against such preference policies, but there is no clear answer to whether such a policy is constitutional.

Some states have a policy to place children with parents of the same ethnic background.

The Birth Certificate

A new birth certificate with the child's adoptive name and the adoptive parents' names is prepared after the adoption is finalized. Generally, at the final hearing, the judge signs a "certificate of adoption" which is sent by the clerk of the court to the state's public records registrar where the child was born. The certificate of adoption provides the state registrar with all the information that is needed to prepare a new birth certificate for the child. The state registrar will then send the adoptive parents an order form so they may order certified copies of the new birth certificate. This process takes usually four to eight weeks depending on what states are involved.

Note: The birth certificate will be issued from the state where the child was born. This may be different than the state where the adoption is finalized.

Confidentiality of the Adoption

Believing that the birth parents and the adoptive parents are entitled to privacy, all states close the records and hearings involved in the adoption to the public. Even the agencies and the attorneys are prevented from disclosing information about the people involved in the adoption.

This confidentiality exists throughout the adoption procedure and afterwards. Some states allow adoption records to be opened with the consent of the birth parents and the adoptive parents. The records also may be opened for "good cause." One example of good cause may be where the adopted person needs a bone marrow donor and a suitable match is not found in the general population.

In some states, the files may now be opened after the child reaches a certain age if the birth parents have given permission. This permission is typically obtained at the time the consent to adopt is signed. Later, if the birth parents change their minds and decide not to allow the file to be opened, they simply need to notify the court or the adoption agency or attorney involved. Refer to Appendix B for an example *Consent to Disclose* form, used in the state of Arizona.

The birth parents may decide at the time they sign the consent that they do not want the file opened and the court will honor this request. If later the birth parents decide that they do want their file to be opened, they can change their mind and let the court, agency or attorney know of their change of heart.

The rules on confidentiality also mean that birth parents and adoptive parents can not find out information about each other without the

The agencies and the attorneys are prevented from disclosing information about the people involved in the adoption.

other's permission. Usually, the information which is prohibited from being disclosed is **identifying information**, information that directly identifies either the birth parents or adoptive parents.

Without disclosing identifying information, the birth parents and the adoptive parents may agree to share information about each other and the child after placement and after the adoption is finalized. Most adoptive parents agree to send pictures of the child and written updates about the child to the birth parents.

Most adoptive parents agree to send pictures of the child and written updates to the birth parents.

Sometimes these updates are sent directly to the birth parents. Sometimes the updates are sent to a go-between, such as an attorney or counselor.

The pictures and updates may give the birth parents comfort that the child is in good care. This helps the birth parents to believe that adoption was the best for the child.

While there is no legal obligation for the adoptive parents to send these updates and pictures, most adoptive parents are very sensitive to the birth parents' needs and therefore honor the birth parents' request for updates. In some situations, for whatever reason, the contact between the birth and adoptive parents is broken. There is also an organization named Search Triad, Inc., which helps birth parents and birth children find each other.

CHAPTER SEVEN
SPECIAL CASE ADOPTIONS

Adopting a Relative's Child

Anyone can adopt a child related to them by blood or marriage. Step-parent adoptions are perhaps the most common example of relative adoptions. But adoptions between an aunt and niece or nephew or a grandparent and grandchild are also common.

Legally speaking, a relative adoption is less complicated than an agency or attorney adoption. For example, in many states, a stepparent, uncle, aunt, or grandparent does not need to be certified or approved to adopt. However, relative adoptions present different emotional issues than non relative adoptions. For example, in a grandparent/grandchild adoption, how does the child refer to his biological mother when his biological relationship to her is one of mother and son and his legal relationship to her is as his sister? These emotional issues should be addressed in counseling.

> *Legally speaking, a relative adoption is less complicated than an agency or attorney adoption.*

Step Parent Adoptions

In a step parent adoption, the prospective adoptive parent is the spouse of one of the natural or adoptive parents of the child. Although a step parent adoption is less complicated than a regular, non relative adoption, the same legal steps will apply. The exception is that a step parent usually does not need to be certified to adopt.

The biological parent and step parent still must file a petition to adopt and provide notice of the hearing to the other birth parent. A consent to the adoption must given by the biological parent bringing the adoption. A consent must be given by the child if the child is over a certain age (usually 12).

More important, unless the child's other parent is deceased, a consent to the adoption must be obtained from this parent. If a consent to adopt cannot be obtained from the other parent, either because the parent refuses or cannot be located, then that person's parental rights must be terminated by a court before the adoption will be granted. As with other adoptions, termination of parental rights requires the parent to be unfit or to have abandoned the child.

Consent to adopt by a birth parent cannot be exchanged for forgiveness of overdue child support.

Abandonment sometimes may be based on the failure to visit the child or to provide child support. However, a consent to adopt by a birth parent with a duty to pay child support can not be exchanged for the forgiveness of overdue child support payments. Such an exchange is considered to be the selling and buying of a child.

Before going forward with a step parent adoption, the parent and step parent should seriously consider whether cutting the child off from one parent is truly in the child's best interest. This is another situation where adoption counseling may be extremely helpful. Consulting with an adoption counselor or psychologist may be helpful in evaluating the child's relationship with the non custodial biological parent and whether terminating this relationship would be beneficial or detrimental to the child.

After the adoption is finalized, the legal relationship between the adopted child and the adoptive step parent changes. They become parent and child, just the same as if the child had been born to the step parent.

Grandparents

Grandparents may adopt their grandchild if the birth parents agree, if the parents are dead, or if the parents have had their parental rights terminated because they are unfit or have abandoned the child. Often, grandparents are not required to be certified or approved to adopt their own grandchildren. Therefore, the adoption process goes much more quickly and easily. Nevertheless an adoption petition and hearing is still required.

Often, grandparents are not required to be certified to adopt their own grandchildren.

Grandparents and great-grandparents are often provided visitation rights to their grandchildren when the grandchildren's parents divorce. Similar visitation rights are not given when the grandchild is been placed for adoption outside the family. Any visitation rights that the grandparents may have enjoyed automatically terminate when the parental rights of the grandchildren's parents are ended. Grandparents are denied visitation in such situations because an adoption decree creates a new family.

Many grandparents are shocked to discover that their rights to their biological grandchildren are so limited. In some states, the grandparent of the adoptive child must consent to the adoption if the parent is a minor. So in these states, a grandparent may block an adoption. Once the child is placed for adoption, the grandparents do not have any further rights to that child.

Grandparents, however, may receive pictures and updates on the adoptive child, **if the adoptive parents agree to this.** This decision is solely up to the adoptive parents.

Adult Adoptions

Many states now have enacted laws allowing adults to be adopted. However, the adoption of adults differs significantly from the adoption of children, both legally and socially.

Adult adoptions differ in that there is usually a shorter waiting period.

Adult adoptions differ legally in that there is usually a shorter waiting period before the adoption is finalized. Also, there may be no requirement for a home study investigation or for a consent to adoption from the birth parents.

Generally for this adoption to be granted, the judge must find that the adoption is in the best interests of the parties and the public interest. For instance, the adoption may be motivated by economic considerations like inheritance, health insurance coverage, etc. Perhaps the adoption is motivated by social concerns like family togetherness.

Some states limit adult adoption to a stepchild, niece, nephew, cousin, or grandchild of the adoption person. Other states have broadened this law to provide for individuals to adopt a friend so that the public will recognize a legal relationship between them.

Special Needs Children

Various factors may define a child as a special needs child. These factors can include racial or ethnic origin, or physical, mental, or developmental disability. If the child is more than six than six years old, the child also may be characterized as a special needs child because of age.

Because of a law passed by the United States Congress, parents who adopt a special needs child may be eligible for an adoption subsidy. Under the Adoption Assistance and Child Welfare Act of 1980, the adoption of special needs children may be subsidized by matching grants between the federal and state governments.

Parents who adopt a special needs child may be eligible for an adoption subsidy.

Essentially the federal law makes all children who are eligible for federal assistance while in foster care, eligible for similar assistance after they are adopted. The goal of the law is to give special needs children a better chance of being placed in a permanent home.

The eligibility criteria for adopting parents are not their financial circumstances, but the circumstances of the child. The circumstances of the child include that the child cannot be returned to the birth parents, that the child is unlikely to be placed for adoption without a subsidy, and that reasonable efforts have been made, without success, to find a placement without providing assistance.

While the financial circumstances of the adoptive parents do not affect their eligibility for an adoption subsidy, they are a factor in considering the amount of benefits.

The Native American Child

Any adoption involving an **Indian child** must follow the **Indian Child Welfare Act of 1978**. An "Indian child" is defined by the Act as "any unmarried person who is under age eighteen and is either: (a) a member of an Indian tribe; or (b) eligible for membership in an Indian tribe and is the biological child of a member of an Indian tribe."

While thousands of people in the United States have some degree of Native American blood, unless a child has at least one parent that is legally entitled to membership in a federally recognized Indian tribe, that child probably cannot qualify for membership. If this is the situation, then the Federal Indian Child Welfare Act does not apply to an adoption.

The Indian Child Welfare Act protects the right of Native American children to grow among their own people.

The Indian Child Welfare Act is a federal law; that is, it applies to the whole country and supersedes any state adoption laws. The purpose of the Indian Child Welfare Act is to protect the right of Native American children to grow among their own people and to teach them to respect their culture and heritage.

Essentially what happens in an Indian adoption is that the tribe takes an active role in the adoption. The tribe must receive notice of the adoption and may have very definite ideas about where the child is placed for adoption. The tribe may prefer that the child be placed as follows:

1) With a member of the Indian child's extended family, including grandparents;

2) With other members of the Indian child's Tribe;

3) With other Indian families.

The tribe's preferences may differ from the birth parents' wishes. The birth parent must either come to some agreement with the tribe as to where the child is placed for adoption or not have the adoption completed.

As has been discussed earlier, consents to adopt will vary from state to state. However, an **Indian consent** will be essentially the same throughout the country. An Indian consent is taken no sooner than ten days following the birth of the child. The consent must be executed in writing before a judge (usually a state court judge) and accompanied by the judge's certificate that the consent was explained in detail and fully understood by the parent. The consent can be revoked; that is the parent can change her mind anytime before the termination of parental rights or the final adoption hearing, whichever comes first.

An Indian ***consent to*** ***adopt*** *will be essentially the same throughout the country.*

Even if the tribe chooses not to intervene in the adoption of an Indian child, and the tribe allows the birth parent to place her child with a non-Indian family, the birth parent must still execute an Indian consent. The adoptive parents must then be made fully aware that the birth parents could change their minds about the adoption **at any time** until a termination is granted or the adoption is final.

CHAPTER EIGHT
ADOPTING A CHILD FROM
OUTSIDE YOUR STATE
••

Adoptive parents in one state may adopt a child from another state. However, in this situation the adoptive parents will need to comply with the **Interstate Compact on the Placement of Children**, sometimes referred to as the ICPC.

The Interstate Compact on the Placement of Children is a general law which all the states and territories of the United States separately have made their law. The ICPC was created to assure proper, safe placements of children between states. Its purpose is to require states to cooperate with each other and make sure that the legal requirements of both states have been followed. One requirement of interstate adoptions is that the adoptive parents must be approved or certified as acceptable adoptive parents before the child is placed with them.

To adopt a child from another state, it is important to be aware of the ICPC and how it works.

If adoptive parents plan to adopt a child from another state, it is extremely important that they and their lawyer be aware of the ICPC and how it works since all the states and territories of the United States follow the ICPC. Every state and United States jurisdiction has a **compact administrator.**

Before a child is brought from one state into another, the compact administrator from each state must be notified. The compact administrator from each state will review the adoption paperwork, and if it is in order, the administrator will allow the child to return with the adoptive parents to their home state.

It is extremely important to realize that until the interstate compact paperwork is approved, the adoptive parents may not leave the state where they received the child to return to their home state. Traveling without the administrator's permission violates the laws of both the state in which they received the child as well as the home state.

Violators are subject to punishment or penalties in both jurisdictions. Actual assessment of penalties has been rare, but since 1980, there have been several cases in which children placed in violation of the ICPC were taken away from the adoptive parents and returned to the child's state.

Even though the adoptive parents may not return to their home state until they receive approval, they may travel anywhere within the boundaries of the state in which they received the baby. Some adoptive parents view the waiting for ICPC approval as a "mini-vacation" and a chance for them to bond with the baby before returning home to the onslaught of enthusiastic friends and relatives.

The approval process sometimes only takes two or three days. Sometimes it can take two to four weeks or longer. The time for ICPC approval depends on the states involved. (Michigan, Virginia, Massachusetts and the District of Columbia typically have longer approval times while Arizona and Indiana are fairly quick.) It is helpful to get a ball park figure of what the anticipated approval time will be before being placed with the child.

There are **exceptions to the Interstate Compact**. The most important one is that some relatives can take a child across state lines without involving the Interstate Compact. Therefore, if there is going to be a relative adoptive placement between two states, there may be no need to involve the Interstate Compact.

Adopting a Child From a Foreign Country

Because of the shortage of adoptable infants in the United States, many American parents are considering adopting foreign children. Adoptive parents can adopt a child from another country through a United States agency which specializes in foreign adoptions or through "direct" adoption.

One of the largest agencies is the Holt Adoption Agency in Eugene, Oregon.

One of the largest international adoption agencies is the Holt Adoption Agency in Eugene, Oregon. This agency is over 35 years old and places foreign children with American families from 15 different countries: Korea, India, Thailand, the Philippines, Vietnam, Hong Kong, Brazil, Cost Rica, Ecuador, Guatemala, Cambodia, Romania, Russia, Ukraine, and the People's Republic of China.

The cost of adopting through this agency varies from country to country as does the time to be placed with a child. Both the cost and time will vary with the type of child desired.

The Holt Agency advises that each country has its own adoption guidelines and different age children are available in different countries.

The adoptive parents will need to complete a home study and may need to transport the child from the foreign country to the United States. The immigration process will need to be completed by the adoptive parents once they return home. Additionally because the Visa and passport process can be lengthy, adoptive parents may wait three to six months after having a child identified before being able to bring the child to the United States.

The alternative to an adoption of a foreign child through an agency is a direct adoption. In this case, the child to be adopted is found by the adoptive parents.

Recent television programs focused on the plight of Romanian children and caused a virtual migration of American adoptive parents to adopt these children. Many parents, once in Romania, learned how complicated and frustrating a foreign adoption can be.

Before going to a foreign country, the adoptive parents must do their homework and be prepared for anything.

Before going to a foreign country, the adoptive parents must do their homework and be prepared for anything. Once in the country, adoptive parents should not expect things to go smoothly. Foreign country have their own laws, customs, money, language, and food.

In preparing to go to the foreign country, adoptive parents should learn as much as they can about the country and its lifestyles. If food and basic necessities are scarce, supplies must be taken. Where and how to exchange money must be learned. The adoptive parents must have a contact person in the country, ideally an attorney or agency, to direct them. (The International Concerns Committee for Children, located in Boulder, Colorado prepares a Report on Foreign Adoptions which contains a listing of agencies that may be contacted to assist with direct adoptions of foreign children.)

Not only will the adoption laws of adoptive parents' state be involved, but so will the laws of the foreign country. Perhaps more critical in the preparation to adopt a foreign child is awareness of the United States immigration procedures.

Generally, to enter the United States, the foreign adoptive child must be an "orphan" as that term is defined by the immigration laws of the United States. If both parents have died or have disappeared or abandoned the children, the child is an orphan. If one parent is available but that parent is not able to care for the orphan properly, the child is an orphan as long as the parent agrees to release the children for immigration and adoption.

To enter the United States, the foreign adoptive child must be an "orphan," as defined by U.S. immigration laws.

In order for the foreign child to immigrate to the United States, an Orphan Petition must be filed. Any United States citizen of any age who is married and any unmarried United States citizen at least 25 years old may file this petition. Once the petition is approved, the child is made a relative of a United States citizen, and is eligible for an immigrant visa without waiting. The child, however, must not have any disqualifying factors, such as a contagious disease.

Along with the Orphan Petition, certain documents must be presented: the fingerprints of the adoptive parents, a favorable home study for the adoptive parents, proof of the child's age by birth certificate or other evidence, death certificates of the child's parents if applicable, evidence that the child's sole surviving parent cannot provide for the child's care or has consented to the child's immigration and adoption, and the final decree of adoption if the child has been adopted abroad.

Much of the immigration paperwork can be done before the adoptive parents travel.

Much of the immigration paperwork can be done before the adoptive parents travel and before the child is even identified. This process is called "Advance Processing". A home study is required and must be included with an advance processing application for orphan petition.

The paperwork required by the U.S. Immigration Service, including the Orphan Petition (Form I-600), may be obtained from any of the United States Immigration and Naturalization Service District Offices. Adoptive parents also should obtain the U.S. Immigration and Naturalization Service's pamphlet titled "The Immigration of Adopted and Prospective Adoptive Children."

CHAPTER NINE
NEW DIRECTIONS
· ·

Open Adoptions

Ten years ago, adoptive parents rarely knew much more about the birth parents of their child than a superficial physical description and some medical history. Some birth parents who placed children for adoption twenty or more years ago did not even know the sex of the child they placed for adoption much less whether their child were alive and well. Adopted children who are now adults may not know why their birth parents placed them for adoption.

Today, much more information is shared between the birth parents and the adoptive parents. They even may agree to an **open adoption**. The term open adoption, however, means different things to different people.

> *Today, much more information is shared between the birth parents and the adoptive parents.*

To some, an open adoption may be a meeting between the birth parents and adoptive parents where only first names are used. To others, an open adoption is one where contact is maintained between the birth and adoptive parents through a third person, like an agency or attorney. And to others open adoption is where names and addresses of the birth and adoptive parents are exchanged and ongoing contact is maintained between the birth parents and the adoptive child.

There are very many variations to these scenarios. It is important for the birth and adoptive parents to define exactly what they mean by an "open adoption" so they do not have different expectations.

An adoption counselor can assist the birth and adoptive parents to define what kind of open adoption is right for both of them. The counselor can help the birth and adoptive parents write down their expectations. This written understanding is beneficial so that both sides understand what is expected of them. It is extremely important that both the birth parents and the adoptive parents understand, however, that this is not a legally enforceable contract. It is rather a moral obligation between the birth parents and the adoptive parents.

A written understanding is beneficial so that both sides understand what is expected of them.

A typical kind of open adoption is one where the birth parents and adoptive parents meet before the birth of the child. Sometimes the birth mother and the adoptive mother go to the obstetrician appointments together and the adoptive mother is present at the delivery of the baby. Then following the placement of the baby with the adoptive parents, the adoptive parents send pictures and written updates on the child to the birth parents. These updates can be sent on any schedule which the parents agree upon, but a schedule which has worked well in the past is to send the updates at one month, three months, six months, one year, eighteen months, two years, then once a year after that.

There are many good things about this new openness to adoptions. Fears and stereotypes are broken down. Many times, adoptive parents fear that their child's birth parent is lurking behind every street corner ready to steal the child. By meeting the birth parents, these fears are usually laid to rest. It is reassuring to meet your child's birth parent and to know that they are people with strengths and weakness like everyone else.

Birth mothers sometimes are stereotyped as immoral girls or unloving mothers. Meeting and knowing the birth mother usually leads to understanding that the woman is just like everyone else. Instead of being an immoral girl, the birth mother may have lived a good life and made one slip in judgment. Instead of being an unloving mother, the birth mother may be making the ultimate loving sacrifice so her child has a better home and life than she could ever offer.

Openness is beneficial for the adoptive child as well. Adoptive children need to know why their birth parents placed them for adoption and who these people were. One child did not know anything about her birth mother, so she made up a story about her. She figured that her mother must have been a promiscuous high school dropout. Upon hearing their daughter describe her birth mother to a friend, the girl's parents revealed that her mother was actually a very religious college honor roll student. Their daughter was very relieved and glad to learn this information about her birth mother. The truth may not always be as pleasant as it was in this example, but most often the truth is more positive than one imagines. In any event, it is oftentimes better to know than not to know.

Adoptive children need to know why their birth parents placed them for adoption.

For the birth parents, too, openness is very positive. Many birth parents need to see pictures of the child and to hear how much the adoptive parents love her. It is a very common worry of the adoptive parents that if the birth parents see pictures of the child, then they will want the child back. Or the adoptive parents fear that by seeing the child, the birth parent will never "get on" with her life. This appears not to be true.

It is very reassuring for the birth parents to see pictures of the child looking happy, healthy and loved. This reaffirms to the birth parent that they made the right decision. This confidence, that they made the right decision, helps the birth parents move on with their life. Without this confidence, the birth parents may reach a crisis situation where they panic and are sure that something is wrong with their child, that the child needs them, and then they may try to find the child. Instead of jeopardizing the bond between the adoptive parents and the child, openness actually can safeguard the adoption.

Instead of jeopardizing the bond, openness actually can safeguard the adoption.

Surrogate Parenting

Surrogate parenting involves a woman who is artificially inseminated and who carries the baby to term with the intention of relinquishing the child at birth to the couple whose husband provided the sperm. With the scarcity of adoptable infants and the technological advances in conception, it is perhaps not surprising that surrogacy is a growing option for infertile couples. Yet this is an area where the technology is surpassing the legislation.

The reaction to the "Baby M" case illustrates this point. This widely publicized case involved a $10,000 surrogacy contract between William and Elizabeth Stern and Mary Beth Whitehead-Gould. The surrogate mother, Mary Beth Whitehead-Gould, was artificially inseminated with William Stern's sperm, agreeing to relinquish the child after birth to the Sterns. Upon delivering the child, Ms. Whitehead-Gould dishonored the surrogacy contract by refusing to place the child with Mr. and Mrs. Stern.

In February, 1988 the New Jersey Supreme Court awarded custody of the 22 month old child to Mr. Stern and granted visitation rights to Ms. Whitehead-Gould. The court said that the surrogacy contract was void, against public policy, and was tantamount to baby selling. The court wrote that "[t]his is the sale of a child, or at the very least, the sale of a mother's right to her child, with the only mitigating factor being that one of the purchasers is the father." The court also stated that the contract failed to consider the best interests of the child, the fitness of the contracting parents, and the impact of separation on the natural mother and child. In short, the surrogacy contract has none of the safeguards of an adoptive placement.

The states are unsettled as to how to handle surrogacy. New laws constantly are being introduced in state legislatures regarding this situation. Without clear laws on the issue, courts may have to decide the rights, if any, of the parties to a surrogacy agreement. It is extremely important that anyone considering surrogate parenting find out what her state's current position is regarding surrogacy.

Without clear laws on the issue, courts may have to decide the rights of the parties to a surrogacy agreement.

Gay Adoptions

The rights of homosexuals to adopt are not at all clear. Even though there are no laws which expressly prevent a homosexual from becoming an adoptive parent, sexual orientation sometimes plays a role in adoption hearings. In determining what is best for the child, the judges sometimes rule that the sexual orientation or activity (a factor equally applicable to either heterosexual or homosexual parents) of the adoptive parent makes the home unsuitable for the child. The clearest statement is that each case depends on its own facts.

Even where adult adoptions are allowed, an adoption between lovers usually is not allowed.

When the person to be adopted is not a child, it must be remembered that many states do not allow adult adoptions under any circumstance. Even where adult adoptions are allowed, an adoption between lovers usually is not allowed. The reasoning for this result is that the purpose of adoption is to create a parent and child relationship, and therefore the procedure should not be used to create another kind of relationship. There are a few states whose statutes do allow for an adoption between adult gays.

Aids and Adoption

Attorneys and agencies, as well as other professionals working in the adoption field, are concerned about the impact AIDS will have upon adoption. Some agencies require testing of all birth mothers, while others only require that high-risk clients be tested. In any event, both attorneys and agencies are probing more deeply to determine whether a client is in a high risk group. Some agencies are focusing primarily on finding foster and adoptive homes for HIV children, and have been successful in locating families who are educated about the problem and able to take special care of these children.

CHAPTER TEN
PRACTICAL CONSIDERATIONS

The Expense of an Adoption

What will it cost to adopt a child? Simple question, but very difficult to answer. There are many kinds of adoptions, and therefore adoptions vary greatly in cost. Some adoptions cost nothing and others exceed $30,000. It is important that potential adoptive parents find out exactly what the agency or attorney will charge and how the money will be spent.

An adoption may indeed cost nothing, if the adoption takes place through a state agency. These adoptions usually involve hard to place children and sometimes the state pays the adoptive parents a subsidy to help take care of the child.

> *An adoption may indeed cost nothing, if the adoption takes place through a state agency.*

Other adoptions may only cost $2,000 to $4,000 if there are very little costs involved in the adoption. For instance, the birth mother's medical expenses are paid by her insurance and her only expenses are adoption counseling and her attorney's fees.

More usual are those adoptions which range from $5,000 to $12,000. Typically, these adoptions cover medical expenses, counseling, certification costs, authorized living expenses, and attorney's fees.

Therefore, the cost of any two adoptions may vary depending on whether the birth mother has medical insurance, whether she needed much adoption counseling, or simply saw a counselor once or not at all. Likewise, the cost of legal fees will be greater if the adoption involved the Interstate Compact, Indian Child Welfare Act, or the termination of parental rights.

Agency fees vary greatly as well. Some agencies receive funding from a church or the United Way and are able to provide lower fees to their clients. Other agencies have a sliding scale fee to help accommodate their clients. Private agencies who receive no funding may rely solely on their clients to pay for all the adoption expenses. As would be expected, these agencies charge higher fees.

In working with an agency, adoptive parents should be sure to find out what the agency fee covers and what additional expenses, if any, they may need to pay.

Services Available for Birth Parents

There are services available to the birth parents before and after the placement of their child. Perhaps the most important service to a birth parent is **adoption counseling**. This counseling is important before the birth of the child and after the birth of the child. Placing a child for adoption is perhaps one of the most difficult and important decisions in a birth parent's life. To place a child for adoption is a lifelong decision. That is why counseling is so important.

Counseling before the baby's birth can help the parents sort out their feelings. Counseling can help them through the process of determining whether adoption is the right decision for them and the baby, or whether another option is best for them.

Talking with friends and family is helpful and important, but it also helps to have a counselor who is experienced with adoption issues to provide a more unbiased and informed viewpoint. Remember, the counselor is paid regardless of whether the adoption occurs; therefore her counseling can be impartial. In most states the counseling expense can be paid for by the adoptive parents.

For a birth mother, counseling is helpful to prepare her for how she might feel following the birth of the child. A mother will undergo dramatic physical, hormonal and emotional changes following the birth of her child. Even in a non adoption situation, when a baby is planned for and all is going well in the mother's life, the new mother may be thrown for a loop after the birth of her child.

For a birth mother, counseling is helpful to prepare her for how she might feel following the birth of the child.

So the situation is even more unsettled when the mother has just delivered a child and is faced with the momentous decision to place this child for adoption. It is helpful then for the mother to be forewarned of how she may feel after the delivery—to know that the emotional roller coaster she is riding is normal.

It is also helpful for the mother to think back to her counseling sessions, and to rely on the decisions she made during counseling when she was thinking clearly and not under the influence of her emotions, hormones or any drugs given to her during delivery or recovery.

Counseling is also helpful **after the placement** of the child. After the placement, it is normal for the birth parent to feel depressed. Even when the birth parents are secure that their decision was the right one, the placement of a child is a loss, and it is normal (and healthy) to go through a grieving process.

Without counseling, some birth parents fear that "there is something wrong with them" and that they "should be getting over this." It is a relief to find out that this is normal and that the pain will ease with time.

Another service available to birth parents are **birth parent support group meetings**. These meetings are for parents who have placed a child for adoption. Placing a child for adoption can be a very lonely experience. Even birth parents, who have confided in friends and family, and whose friends and family have been very supportive of them, can feel isolated. It is helpful to talk with other birth parents whose personal experiences allow them to truly understand another birth mother's feelings.

For those birth parents who have kept their adoption secret, the support group meetings can be extremely important.

For those birth parents who have kept their adoption secret, the support group meetings can be extremely important. At last they will have a safe place to talk about their adoption. To find a birth parent support group, a birth parent may contact an adoption agency, a local adoption attorney, or a counseling center for referral.

Search Triad, Inc. is an organization offering help to birth parents and adoptive children who are searching for their birth child or birth parent. Its goal is to reunite families separated by adoption, foster care or divorce. The organization provides trained search assistants and library resources to aid in this search. The services of Search Triad will be more useful in an adoption which took place years ago, before there was any information available about the adoption.

Arizona has recently enacted a Confidential Intermediary Program administered by the Arizona Supreme Court. The Confidential Intermediary may release confidential information to the birth parents and the adult adoptive child if all parties concerned consent to the release of information.

Services Available for Adoptive Parents

As with birth parents, there are services available for adoptive parents before and after the placement of their child.

Adoptive parents just starting the adoption process may want to contact an organization called Resolve. Resolve is a nonprofit support group established by individuals who have been touched by infertility. Resolve offers monthly meetings to discuss medical treatments for infertility as well as other options such as adoption.

Adoption education may be the most beneficial service available to adoptive parents.

Adoption education, however, may be the most beneficial service available to adoptive parents. Raising a child, whether it is a birth child or an adoptive child, is mostly universal. All parents—regardless of how they came to be parents—will need to deal with teething, ear infections, school plays and whether or when to give the child a puppy.

But there is a difference when explaining how you became a family. And the issue of birth parents must be explained to the child. Life did not just begin for your child at the moment of placement. Your child has a history which predates you and it is important to know how to share that information with your child.

It is for situations like this that **adoption education** can be extremely beneficial. Adoption education can teach adoptive parents how and when to tell the child about her adoption. Adoptive parents will become more aware of what questions their child is likely to ask, at what age. Usually the more educated the adoptive parents are about the adoption process, the less frightened they will be about it. This is truly a situation where knowledge is confidence.

This kind of education ought to be helpful in fielding some of the well-meaning, but tactless statements as, "Well, now you'll get pregnant and have your **own** child." This education also may break down some of the prejudices and misconceptions about adoption, such as the mistaken belief that the adoptive parents are not the child's **real** parents or the myth that the child may be the product of "bad seed."

Adoption education may provide the opportunity to meet with other adoptive parents in a situation similar to child birth classes. It is always comforting to meet people who are in the same situation, others who know how difficult it is to wait for a baby or who have had the experience of a match falling through.

Many adoption programs offer the opportunity to meet with birth parents, grown adoptive children and adoptive parents. It is a great opportunity to be able to view adoption from all sides and it provides a better understanding of what the concerns of all parties are in an adoption.

Adoption education is an ongoing process. When the child is a teenager, new questions may emerge and the adoptive parents may feel a need for more education. They should feel free to contact the adoption agency or adoption counselor for more education.

Adoption agencies, adoption attorneys, or local counseling centers can provide referrals and information on adoption education. If there is not a support group in your area, consider starting one!

Parenting Classes

Bringing a new baby home from the hospital is nerve wracking. However, adoptive parents will feel a lot more comfortable if they have had some experience. If the adoptive parents did not spend their teenage years baby sitting all the children on the block, they ought to consider taking a parenting class. Otherwise they may find themselves at 1 o'clock at night trying to read the directions on the box of diapers to know which way the tabs stick, while the baby is howling at their incompetence.

Most parenting classes offer baby sitting services too!

Most hospitals offer parenting classes or can provide referrals.

When adopting an older child, adoptive parents may find parenting classes particularly helpful if they can find a class which deals with children of their child's age group. Most parenting classes offer baby sitting services too!

CHAPTER ELEVEN
DISRUPTED ADOPTIONS

Sadly, not all adoptive placements work out. There are two basic types of **adoption disruptions**:

1) Where the child is removed from the adoptive parents' home, and

2) Where the adoptive parents ask that the child be removed from their home.

Involuntary Disruption

There are several reasons why the first kind of disruption, the removal of the child from the adoptive parents' home, may occur. There may be a fatal flaw in the consent to adopt. For instances, perhaps the consent was signed too early and therefore is invalid. If this were true, then the birth parent could challenge the consent and have the child returned.

Perhaps the birth father's rights were ignored. If the birth father never signed a consent to adopt and his rights were never terminated in a court proceeding, the birth father could prove that he was the father, make a successful claim for his child, and disrupt the adoption.

If the birth father's rights were ignored, he could make a successful claim for the child and disrupt the adoption.

It also happens, though, that the child is not doing well in the adoptive parents' home. During the time between the placement of the child and the finalization of the adoption, a caseworker will meet with the adoptive parents and the child. If the caseworker believes that the child is not being cared for properly in the home, the child may be removed and the adoption disrupted. **If this happens, the adoptive parents should consult immediately with an attorney to find out their rights and liabilities.**

Voluntary Disruption

In the second situation, the adoptive parents wish to have the child removed from their home and the adoption disrupted. In some cases, the adoptive parents believed themselves ready and willing to be parents, but after a period of time, they realize they do not want to be parents and want to return the child to the agency or attorney. Ideally, this should not happen if the adoptive parents were certified to adopt and received adoption counseling. But it sometimes does happen.

In other cases, the child develops problems that the adoptive parents feel they are unable to handle. These problems may be emotional or physical problems, or even it may be that the child "looks different" than the adoptive parents expected. Whatever the reason, the adoptive parents **can** return the child **so long as the adoption has not been finalized**.

Once the adoption has been finalized, it is uncertain whether the child can be returned.

Once the adoption has been finalized, it is uncertain whether the child can be returned. Some adoptive parents have been successful in removing the child from their home upon showing that they were not given important background history on the child.

In a precedent-setting case from Ohio, the Ohio Supreme Court sided with the adoptive parents in a **wrongful adoption** lawsuit against a county adoption agency. The court determined that the agency told the adoptive parents that the child was healthy even though the agency was aware of tests showing that the child may have low intelligence and was at risk of disease. The court awarded the adoptive parents $125,000. The court decided:

"[i]t would be a travesty of justice and a distortion of the truth to conclude that deceitful placement of this infant, known by [the agency] to be at risk, was not actionable when the tragic but hidden realities of the child's infirmities finally came to light." The court went on to state that "[i]n no way do we imply that adoption agencies are guarantors of their placements. Such a view would be tantamount to imposing an untenable contract of insurance that each child adopted would mature to be healthy and happy . . . However, just as couples must weigh the risks of becoming natural parents, taking into consideration a host of factors, so too should adoptive parents be allowed to make their decision in an intelligent manner. It is not mere failure to disclose the risks inherent in this child's background which we hold actionable. Rather, it is the deliberate act of misinforming this couple which deprived them of their right to make a sound parenting decision and which led to the compensable injuries."

But this is a very troublesome area. It must be remembered that a child is a life, not a commodity with a guarantee. Probably the strongest case for a disrupted adoption after the

It must be remembered that a child is a life, not a commodity with a guarantee.

adoption is finalized is where some fraud or misrepresentation is involved about the medical or social history of the child. Courts in Minnesota, California, Wisconsin, and Pennsylvania recently have followed the decision of the Ohio Supreme Court.

The adoptive parents must understand the child's situation and be willing to love and accept that child as is.

Perhaps the best safeguard against this kind of adoption disruption is to receive as much background history as possible about the birth parents. At no time should information be withheld from the adoptive parents. The adoptive parents must understand the child's situation and be willing to love and accept that child as is.

Truthful and total disclosure with education is the best way to deal with these situations. If the child is a result of incest or rape, adoptive parents may be willing to accept this. If the child was abused or sexually molested, adoptive parents ought to receive education about what this history might mean to the child, what behaviors the child may exhibit as a result of this and how to cope. If the child is a drug baby, the adoptive parents must be informed as to what kinds of effects the drugs may have on the child both short and long term as well as how to comfort the child during the withdrawal stage.

APPENDIX A

BIRTH MOTHER BACKGROUND INFORMATION

Physical Description:

Height _____ Hair texture _____
Weight _____ Complexion _____
Eye color _____ Build _____
Hair color _____ Right or left handed _____

At what age did you do the following:

Turn over _____ Stand _____
Sit _____ Walk _____
Crawl _____ Talk _____

Description of personality (e.g. happy, high-strung, easy-going, moody, morning person, etc.):

_____

_____

Ethnic background:

_____

Date of birth _____ Primary language _____
Birthplace _____ Religion _____

Marital status (include dates and places of marriages, divorces):

_____

_____

Relationship between birth parents (married, divorced, separated, living together, widowed):

_____

_____

Are you a member of an Indian Tribe? If yes, which one?

_____

BIRTH MOTHER BACKGROUND, CONTINUED

Other Children (sex, birthdates, health and physical condition and current whereabouts—e.g. residing with parent, in foster home, etc.):

1. _____

_____

2. _____

_____

3. _____

_____

4. _____

_____

How many years did you attend school?

_____

What was your scholastic performance?

_____

What were your favorite subjects?

_____

What are your plans for the future? (e.g., work, education, marriage and children):

_____

_____

What are your hobbies, interests or special talents? (e.g., music, art, sports, mechanical, any awards received?)

_____

_____

What is your employment history?

_____

_____

Have you ever been arrested? If yes, please give details.

_____

_____

BIRTH MOTHER BACKGROUND, CONTINUED

Significant childhood events (i.e., was your childhood happy, did you move a lot, did your parents divorce?)

_____

_____

What is your relationship with your parents; are they aware of your adoption plan?

_____

_____

What is your relationship with your siblings; are they aware of your adoption plan?

_____

Please answer the following questions about *your mother:*

Height _____ Hair texture _____

Weight _____ Complexion _____

Eye color _____ Build _____

Hair color _____ Right or left handed _____

Description of personality (e.g. happy, high-strung, easy-going, moody, morning person, etc.)

_____

Age (or age at death) _____

Ethnic background _____

Please answer the following questions about *your father:*

Height _____ Hair texture _____

Weight _____ Complexion _____

Eye color _____ Build _____

Hair color _____ Right or left handed _____

Description of personality (e.g. happy, high-strung, easy-going, moody, morning person, etc.)

_____

Age (or age at death) _____

Ethnic background _____

BIRTH MOTHER BACKGROUND, CONTINUED

Please answer the following questions about your *brother or sister:*
(circle either **brother** or **sister**, whichever is applicable)

Height _____ Hair texture _____

Weight _____ Complexion _____

Eye color _____ Build _____

Hair color _____ Right or left handed _____

Description of personality (e.g. happy, high-strung, easy-going, moody, morning person, etc.)

_____

Age (or age at death) _____

Ethnic background _____

Was anyone in your family adopted? Who?

_____

Why are you placing the child for adoption?

_____

Are you interested in future contact with the child?

_____

Have you had any psychological counseling? Have you had any adoption counseling?

_____

_____

Prenatal Information

Date first seen by a doctor for this pregnancy _____

Weight gained during this pregnancy _____

Age at time of this delivery _____

Number of other pregnancies _____

Number of other live births _____

RH factor _____ Blood type _____

Medications, drugs and alcohol used **before** this pregnancy

_____

_____

BIRTH MOTHER BACKGROUND, CONTINUED

Medications, drugs and alcohol used **during** this pregnancy

_____

_____

Did you take vitamins? If yes, what month did you start?

_____

_____

Please check whether you had any of the following during your pregnancy

German Measles _____ Threatened abortion _____
X-Ray treatment _____ Vaginal bleeding _____
Exposure to chemicals, dust or fumes _____

If yes, please explain

_____

Complications, accidents, or indications of anemia during this pregnancy

_____

_____

Did you have any surgery during this pregnancy? If yes, please give details

_____

_____

Medical History

Please review the following carefully and indicate whether you, **or another blood relative of your family**, have any of the following conditions. If yes, please include the date of onset, treatment, medication and prognosis, etc. Try to be as detailed as possible.

Circulatory System Diseases

Rheumatic fever _____
Heart trouble _____
High blood pressure _____
Stroke _____
Heart attack _____
Other (specify) _____

92

Respiratory System Diseases

    Sinusitis _____

    Hay fever _____

    Allergies _____

    Asthma _____

    Tuberculosis _____

    Emphysema _____

    Cystic fibrosis _____

    Other (specify) _____

Digestive System Diseases

    Ulcer _____

    Gall bladder _____

    Other (specify) _____

Dental Problems

    Cavities _____

    Root canals _____

    Braces _____

    Crowns _____

Urinary System Diseases

    Kidney stones _____

    Bladder infections _____

    Other (specify) _____

Skin Diseases

    Eczema _____

    Dermatitis _____

    Other (specify) _____

Muscle Disorders

    Muscular Dystrophy _____

    Other (specify) _____

Bones/Connective Tissues Disorders

    Arthritis, rheumatism _____

    Scoliosis _____

    Spina Bifida _____

Lupus _____

Other (specify) _____

Nervous System Diseases

Multiple Sclerosis _____

Seizures, epilepsy _____

Parkinson's Disease _____

Sense organ disorders

Color blindness _____

Hearing loss _____

Ear infections _____

Night blindness _____

Wears glasses _____

Other (specify) _____

Blood Diseases

Sickle cell anemia _____

Anemia _____

Hemophilia _____

Other (specify) _____

Cancers (specify type, location, treatment age at onset and prognosis, if known)

_____

_____

Endocrine and Metabolic Disorders

Diabetes _____

Thyroid _____

Phenylketonuria (PKU) _____

Other (specify) _____

Birth Defects

Club foot _____

Heart defect _____

Cleft palate _____

Cerebral palsy _____

Down syndrome _____

Other (specify) _____

BIRTH MOTHER BACKGROUND, CONTINUED

Sexually Transmitted Diseases

Syphilis _____

Gonorrhea _____

Herpes _____

AIDS _____

HIV carrier _____

Hepatitis _____

Mental Disorders

Retardation _____

Schizophrenia _____

Bipolar _____

Severe depression _____

Suicidal _____

Other (specify) _____

Complications of Pregnancy/Childbirth

Miscarriage _____

Premature birth _____

Stillbirth _____

Multiple births _____

Infant deaths/SIDS _____

Other Miscellaneous Disorders

Speech disorders _____

Anorexia, bulimia _____

Learning disability _____

Alcoholism _____

Drug dependency _____

Cerebral palsy _____

Any other conditions you think are important to know

_____

_____

_____

_____

GLOSSARY

Adoptee A person who has been adopted.

Adoption The legal process by which a child becomes the legal child of the adoptive parent(s) just as if that child had been born to them.

Adoption Agency An organization created to assist birth parents and adoptive parents with the placement of children for adoption. Agencies created and run by the government are public agencies. Other agencies are private agencies. Some agencies are operated or sponsored by churches or similar organization and are not designed to make a profit. Some private adoption agencies are operated for a profit.

Birth Parent The biological parent of the child, often referred to as the natural parent. As a matter of adoption law, this is not the child's "real" parent. The "real" parent is the one with the legal rights and responsibilities to the child and that person is the adoptive parent.

Bonding A process over time where the adoptive parents and child develop strong emotional ties.

Certification The investigation made of prospective adoptive parents to make sure that they are suitable adoptive parents. The investigation is conducted and a recommendation is made as to whether or not the applicants are acceptable. In some states this is called the "Home Study."

Consent to Adoption The consent is a legal document whereby the birth parents give up their parental rights to adoptive parents or to an adoption agency. Sometimes referred to as a "surrender" or a "relinquishment."

Decree of Adoption After all of the legal procedures required for the adoption are completed and the required waiting period has expired, the court enters an order, usually known as a decree, or judgment of adoption. This decree finalizes the adoption proceedings and establishes a relationship of parent and child between the adoptive parents and the adoptive child.

Disrupted Adoptions There are two basic types of adoption disruptions: 1) where the child is removed from the adoptive parents' home, and 2) where the adoptive parents ask that the child be removed from their home.

Entitlement A process where adoptive parents develop the sense of deserving a child.

Home Study The investigation made of prospective adoptive parents to make sure that they are suitable adoptive parents. The investigation is conducted and a recommendation is made as to whether or not the applicants are acceptable. In some states this process is called "Certification."

ICPC A statutory law passed by all 50 states and jurisdictions. The primary purpose of the Interstate Compact on the Placement of Children is to provide protection for children involved in a placement between states. The ICPC provides a procedure to follow when such a placement is made and allows the sending state a means to monitor that placement after it has been made.

ICWA The Indian Child Welfare Act is a federal law; that is, it applies to the whole country and supersedes any state adoption laws. The purpose of the ICWA is to protect the right of Indian children to grow among their own people and to teach them to respect their culture and heritage.

Indian Child Any unmarried person who is under age eighteen and is either (a); a member of an Indian tribe or (b) eligible for membership in an Indian tribe and is the biological child of a member of an Indian tribe.

Infertility Inability to conceive or carry a pregnancy to term. It is important to deal with infertility issues prior to placement, as an adoption will not heal all the "hurts" of infertility.

Irrevocable Something that may not changed, revoked or undone. In the adoption context, this term is discussed in relation to the consent to adopt usually signed by the birth parent.

Match This is said to occur when the birth parents and adoptive parents tentatively agree to an adoption involving each other. The match follows the exchange of social and medical background information between the birth and adoptive parents. In dealing with the adoption of new born children, a match may occur long before the child is born.

Non-Identifying Information Background information on the birth parents and adoptive parents which does not identify them. Examples of identifying information include names and addresses, or excessively specific information.

Notice In an adoption proceeding, the adoptive parents must give notice to the parties (the birth parents) against whom the proceeding is being brought However, when a birth parent executes a consent, service of process may be waived. If service of process is not waived, then notice is required. The form of the notice, the method of service, and the time allotted for the birth parent to respond to the notice vary from state to state. Where the identity and/or location of birth parent is unknown, most adoption acts provide for notice by publication in a newspaper.

Open Adoption The sharing of identifying information between the parties, meetings between the birth and adoptive parents, and various agreements for ongoing contact between birth and adoptive parents.

Placement When the adoptive parents actually receive physical custody of the child, the placement has occurred.

Relinquishment The relinquishment is a legal document whereby the birth parents give up their parental rights to adoptive parents or to an adoption agency. Sometimes referred to as a "surrender" or a "consent to adoption."

Severance The legal process by which a birth parent's legal rights and responsibilities to the birth child are severed. Also referred to as the termination of parental rights.

Surrogate gestational mother A woman who carries to delivery a child to which she is not genetically related with the intention of relinquishing the child at birth.

Surrogate mother A woman who is artificially inseminated and carries the baby to term with the intention of relinquishing the child at birth in accordance with a prearranged contract.

Surrender The surrender is a legal document whereby the birth parents give up their parental rights to adoptive parents or to an adoption agency. Sometimes referred to as a "consent to adoption" or a "relinquishment."

Termination The legal process by which a birth parent's legal rights and responsibilities to the birth child are severed. Also referred to as a severance of parental rights.

Traditional adoption Adoptions where birth parents are provided the opportunity to participate in the decision making process, plan for the child, and share information while protecting confidentiality. Also referred to as "confidential" adoptions or "closed adoptions."

Triad Refers to the three sides in an adoption: the birth parents, adoptive parents and the adoptee.

SUGGESTED READING LIST

Adoption: A Handful of Hope, by Suzanne Arms; Celestial Arts Publishers ©1990

The Adoption Triangle, by Arthur Sorosky, Annette Baron, Reuben Pannor; Anchor Press, ©1978

I Am Adopted, by Susan Lapsley; Bradbury Press ©1974

Helping Children Cope with Separation and Loss, by Claudia Jewett

Raising Adopted Children, by Lois Ruskai Melina; Harper & Row ©1986

Lost and Found, by Betty Jean Lifton; Harper & Row ©1987

How Babies and Families are Made, by Patricia Schaffer; Tabor Sarah Books ©1988

The Way Mothers Are, by Miriam Schlein

Dear Birthmother, by Kathleen Silber and Phylis Speedlin; Corona Publishing Company ©1982

RESOURCES

American Academy of
Adoption Attorneys
Post Office Box 33053
Washington, D.C. 20033

Adoption Beginnings (a non-agency networking service)
Jan Walton
(602)838-8292

Holt International Children's
Services
P.O. Box 2880; 1195 City View
Eugene, Oregon 97402
(503)687-2202

International Soundex
Reunion Registry
Post Office Box 2312
Carson City, Nevada 89702
(702)882-7755

RESOLVE; National Office
1310 Broadway
Somerville, MA 02144
(617)623-0744

Search Triad, Inc.
Post Office Box 8055
Phoenix, Arizona 85066
(602)977-1320

APPENDIX B

CONSENT TO ADOPT

IN THE SUPERIOR COURT OF THE STATE OF ARIZONA
IN AND FOR THE COUNTY OF MARICOPA

In the matter of:	) No. _____
	)
BABY DOE	) CONSENT OF NATURAL
	) MOTHER TO ADOPTION
	)
	)
A person under 18 years of age	)

I, BIRTH MOTHER, being the natural mother of BABY DOE, born on _____, 1993, at ___.m., in Phoenix, Maricopa County, Arizona, do hereby relinquish and give up all of my rights to the care, custody, control and visitation of said minor child to JOHN and JANE, husband and wife, for the purpose of adoption. I understand that these are only their first names; however, the adoptive parents are currently certified in the State of Arizona as acceptable to adopt children. I do not wish to know their whole names and I have been furnished with all of the information I wish to know about the adoptive parents. I hereby consent that JOHN and JANE may adopt the minor child. This consent to adoption of the minor child is being signed more than seventy-two (72) hours after the birth of said child. It is being signed in front of a Notary Public.

I understand that this consent is irrevocable and that I cannot change my mind; I am aware that the consent to adoption cannot be withdrawn without a court order. The consent is signed by me freely and voluntarily, without any fraud, duress, coercion or undue influence, and I am acting in a sound mind and memory. I also know that I cannot be directly or indirectly compensated for giving this consent to place my child for adoption, except for reasonable and necessary expenses that I have incurred in connection with the adoption.

I further understand that upon entry of the decree of adoption, the relationship of parent and child, and all the legal rights, privileges, duties, obligations and other legal consequences of the natural relationship of parent and child, including the right of inheritance, shall thereafter exist between BABY DOE and JOHN and JANE. They will be the child's parents. I am also aware that upon the entry of the decree of adoption, the

CONSENT TO ADOPT, CONTINUED

relationship of parent and child between BABY DOE and me shall end and be completely severed and all the legal consequences of the relationship, including the right of inheritance, shall cease to exist. I will no longer be the child's parent.

I further state that I am married and was married at the time of conception. The name, address and whereabouts of the father of said child is BIRTH FATHER, who resides at _____ .

I further consent to and authorize JOHN and JANE, husband and wife, to have the right to consent to necessary medical procedures for the child, and to have the responsibility to provide proper care and support of the child.

I hereby waive, and do not want, any notice of any further adoption and severance proceedings.

SIGNED this _____ day of _____ , 199_, at the hour of _____ .m.

_____

Birth Mother

STATE OF ARIZONA   )
)   ss.
County of Maricopa   )

SUBSCRIBED AND SWORN to before me this _____ day of _____ , 199_, by BIRTH MOTHER.

_____

Notary Public

_____

Street Address

_____

City, State and Zip Code

My Commission Expires:

_____

PETITION TO TERMINATE PARENTAL RIGHTS

IN THE SUPERIOR COURT OF THE STATE OF ARIZONA
IN AND FOR THE COUNTY OF MARICOPA

In the matter of:	) No. _____
	)
BABY DOE	) PETITION TO TERMINATE
	) PARENTAL RIGHTS
	)
	)
A person under 18 years of age	)

Petitioners JOHN and JANE SMITH, through their attorney, hereby allege that to their best information and belief:

1. Petitioners, JOHN and JANE SMITH, reside at _____ _____ .

2. BABY DOE, a male/female child, was born on _____ at Phoenix, Arizona, and currently resides with the prospective adoptive parents, JOHN and JANE SMITH.

3. The Court has jurisdiction in this matter for the reason that the child is present in the State of Arizona.

4. Petitioners, JOHN and JANE SMITH are not related to the minor child.

5. The natural mother of the child is _____ , whose date of birth is _____ , who resides at _____ .

6. Petitioners, JOHN A   and JANE SMITH, have physical custody of the child and are acting in loco parentis to the child.

7. The grounds on which termination of the parent-child relationship is sought are:

    a. That the natural mother, _____ , has relinquished her rights to the subject minor child to Petitioners in accordance with Arizona Revised Statutes Section 8-533(B)(5) by executing a written consent to place the child for adoption, the original of which is attached to this Petition.

    b. That the natural father, _____ , has abandoned the subject minor child or made no effort to maintain the parental relation-

PETITION TO TERMINATE PARENTAL RIGHTS, CONTINUED

ship with the child since its placement or for an excess of six months in accordance with Arizona Revised Statutes Section 8-533(B)(1).

8.   Legal custody of the child should be with the Petitioners, JOHN and JANE SMITH.

9.   Termination of the parent-child relationship between the child and the natural mother, _____ , and the natural father, _____ , JOHN DOE or anyone claiming to be the father of BABY DOE, is in the child's best interest as there is a current adoptive plan for the minor child.

WHEREFORE, Petitioners pray that this Court set a time and place for the hearing on this petition; that notice of the hearing be served on all interested persons or entities as required by law; that this Court enter an order terminating the parent-child relationship between _____ , the natural mother and _____ , JOHN DOE or anyone claiming to be the natural father of BABY DOE, and that this Court make such provisions as the Court may deem just and proper.

DATED this ___ day of _____ , 199 ___

Attorney for Petitioners

By _____

Attorney for Petitioners

VERIFICATION

JOHN and JANE SMITH, being first duly sworn, upon their oath, depose and say:

That they are the prospective adoptive parents of BABY DOE, and therefore authorized to make this Verification; that they have read the forgoing Petition for Termination of Parental Rights of Natural Parents and know the contents thereof; that the same are true of their own knowledge except as to those matters therein stated upon information and belief, and as to those, they believe them to be true.

By _____
                JOHN SMITH

By _____
                JANE SMITH

SUBSCRIBED AND SWORN TO before me this _____ day of _____ , 199_ , by JOHN SMITH.

By _____
                Notary Public

SUBSCRIBED AND SWORN TO before me this _____ day of _____ , 199_ , by JANE SMITH.

By _____
                Notary Public

My Commission Expires:

_____

PETITION TO ADOPT

IN THE SUPERIOR COURT OF THE STATE OF ARIZONA
IN AND FOR THE COUNTY OF MARICOPA

In the matter of:) No. _____

BABY GIRL DOE   ) PETITION TO ADOPT

A Person under 18 years of age   )

Your petitioners, JOHN SMITH and JANE SMITH, husband and wife, respectfully represent as follows:

1. Petitioners are husband and wife, and were married on _____ at _____ .

2. Petitioners, JOHN SMITH, born on _____ , and JANE SMITH, born on _____ , are more than 18 years old.

3. Petitioners reside at _____ .

4. Petitioners desire to adopt the above-named minor child born on _____ , at _____ .

5. Said child is living in the home of Petitioners and such placement was made on _____ , by a direct placement from the birth mother.

6. Petitioners are not related to said child.

7. A Certificate of Acceptability to Adopt was issued in favor of Petitioners on _____ .

8. A full disclosure of fees will be included in the Verified Accounting required to be filed with the Court and the Arizona Department of Economic Security pursuant to Arizona Revised Statutes Section 8-1114.

9. The above-named child does not own any property.

10. All consents necessary to this adoption are filed herein. A Petition to Terminate the natural father's parental rights has been filed with this Court.

WHEREFORE, your Petitioners pray that a time and place for hearing this Petition be set, and for an Order of your Court that the

PETITION TO ADOPT, CONTINUED

undersigned Petitioners have adopted the minor child, that the name of the child shall be changed to _____ , and that henceforth, such child shall be regarded and treated in all respects as the child of your Petitioners.

DATED this _____ day of _____ , 199 ___ .

_____
Attorney for Petitioners

_____
JOHN SMITH

_____
JANE SMITH

State of Arizona   )
)
County of Maricopa   )

JOHN SMITH, being duly sworn, upon his oath, deposes and says:

That he is the Petitioner in the within Petition for Adoption of minor BABY GIRL DOE, that he has read the forgoing Petition and knows the contents thereof; that the same are true of his own knowledge except as to those matters therein stated upon information and belief, and as to those, he believes them to be true.

By _____
      JOHN SMITH

JANE SMITH, being duly sworn, upon her oath, deposes and says:

That she is the Petitioner in the within Petition for Adoption of minor BABY GIRL DOE, that she has read the forgoing Petition and knows the contents thereof; that the same are true of her own knowledge except as to those matters therein stated upon information and belief, and as to those, she believes them to be true.

By _____
      JANE SMITH

SUBSCRIBED AND SWORN TO before me this _____ day of _____ , 199 ___ by JOHN SMITH and by JANE SMITH.

By _____
My commission expires: _____   Notary Public

108

CONSENT TO DISCLOSE INFORMATION

IN THE SUPERIOR COURT OF THE STATE OF ARIZONA
IN AND FOR THE COUNTY OF MARICOPA

In the matter of:	) No. _____
	) AFFIDAVIT OF BIRTH
BABY BOY DOE	) PARENT REGARDING
	) CONSENT TO CHILD'S
	) ACCESS OF ADOPTION
A person under 18 years of age	) RECORDS

I, BIRTH MOTHER, have signed a Consent to Adoption placing my child with certified adoptive parents, JOHN and JANE, for the purposes of adoption.

I hereby grant/withhold (cross out whichever does not apply) my consent for the adopted child, upon reaching the age of 21 years, to review records pertaining to his adoption. I further give permission for the Court and my attorney to release any and all information, including identifying information, about me to my child, upon request, provided my child is at least 21 years of age at the time the request is made.

I realize that this decision to grant/withhold consent to release information may be changed at any time by filing a notarized statement with the Court or my attorney.

SIGNED this _____ day of _____ , 1993 at the hour of _____

_____
Birth Mother

SUBSCRIBED AND SWORN to before me this _____ day of _____ , 1993 , by BIRTH MOTHER.

My Commission Epires:

_____
Notary Public

_____
Street Address

_____   _____
                                            City, State and Zip Code

Index

A

Abandonment, 48-49, 56-57
(see also Birth parents,
  termination of parental
  rights)
Abortion, 16-17
Adoption
  by gay couples, 73-74
  by relative, 12-13, 55,
  by step-parent, 55
  confidentiality of, 34, 52-53
  consequences of informal
    adoption, 1
  costs, 10, 27-30, 74-75
  counseling, 8, 11, 34, 55,
    56, 75-78
  definition, 1
  difference in law by
    country, 67
  differences in state law, 2-
    3, 5, 16, 25, 28, 58, 61,
    67, 74
  direct, 65-68
  disrupted, 83-86
  education, 8, 79-81, 86
  federal law, 3, 59-60
  final decree of adoption,
    13, 51-52, 57, 68
  foreign, 65-68
  formal procedure, 1, 10,
    19-20, 41-54
  hearing, 29, 43, 49-52, 57, 73

  history of, 2-3
  interstate, 63-65
  of adults, 5, 58, 74
  open, 25, 35, 69-74
  prejudices, 80
  reasons for, 2, 58
  types of, 7-13
  waiting period, 5, 13, 41,
    50, 58
Adoption agencies
  advantage of, 8-9
  available services, 8, 76
  deceitful placement of
    infants, 85-86
  differences in criteria, 4, 9
  disadvantage of, 9
  fees/expenses, 27-29, 65, 76
  financial responsibility for
    birth mother, 33
  for profit, 8
  international, 65
  nonprofit private, 8
  private, 7, 9
  public, 3, 7, 9, 75, 85
  role of agency attorney, 9-10
  role in obtaining information
    about birth parents, 25, 74
  state licensing statues, 8
Adoption Assistance and
  Child Welfare Act of 1980, 59
Adoption attorney,
  qualifications, 11-12, 21
  fees, 12, 27